SHAKESPEARE AND BRECHT

ARDEN PERFORMANCE COMPANIONS

Series Editors: Michael Dobson, Abigail Rokison-Woodall and Simon Russell Beale

Published titles

Shakespeare and Lecoq by Ed Woodall and Abigail Rokison-Woodall
Shakespearean Rhetoric by Benet Brandreth
Shakespeare and Stanislavsky by Annie Tyson
'You' and 'Thou' in Shakespeare by Penelope Freedman
Shakespeare and Meisner by Aileen Gonsalves and Tracy Irish

Further titles in preparation

Shakespeare and Laban by Jacquelyn Bessell and Laura Weston

ARDEN PERFORMANCE EDITIONS

Series Editors: Michael Dobson, Abigail Rokison-Woodall and Simon Russell Beale

Published titles

A Midsummer Night's Dream edited by Abigail Rokison-Woodall
As You Like It edited by Nora Williams
Hamlet edited by Abigail Rokison-Woodall
King Lear edited by Simon Russell Beale and Abigail Rokison-Woodall
Macbeth edited by Katherine Brokaw

Much Ado About Nothing edited by Anna Kamaralli
Othello edited by Paul Prescott
Romeo and Juliet edited by Abigail Rokison-Woodall
Richard III edited by Abigail Rokison-Woodall and Simon Russell Beale
The Tempest edited by Miranda Fay Thomas
The Winter's Tale edited by Robert Shaughnessy
Twelfth Night edited by Gretchen Minton

SHAKESPEARE AND BRECHT

A Practical Guide for Actors, Directors, Students and Teachers

Stephen Unwin

THE ARDEN SHAKESPEARE
LONDON • NEW YORK • OXFORD • NEW DELHI • SYDNEY

THE ARDEN SHAKESPEARE
Bloomsbury Publishing Plc, 50 Bedford Square, London, WC1B 3DP, UK
Bloomsbury Publishing Inc, 1359 Broadway, New York, NY 10018, USA
Bloomsbury Publishing Ireland, 29 Earlsfort Terrace, Dublin 2, D02 AY28, Ireland

BLOOMSBURY, THE ARDEN SHAKESPEARE and the Arden Shakespeare logo are trademarks of Bloomsbury Publishing Plc

First published in Great Britain 2025

Copyright © Stephen Unwin, 2025

Stephen Unwin has asserted his right under the Copyright, Designs and Patents Act, 1988, to be identified as author of this work.

Series design by Charlotte Daniels
Cover image: letoosen/Adobe Stock

All rights reserved. No part of this publication may be: i) reproduced or transmitted in any form, electronic or mechanical, including photocopying, recording or by means of any information storage or retrieval system without prior permission in writing from the publishers; or ii) used or reproduced in any way for the training, development or operation of artificial intelligence (AI) technologies, including generative AI technologies. The rights holders expressly reserve this publication from the text and data mining exception as per Article 4(3) of the Digital Single Market Directive (EU) 2019/790.

Bloomsbury Publishing Plc does not have any control over, or responsibility for, any third-party websites referred to or in this book. All internet addresses given in this book were correct at the time of going to press. The author and publisher regret any inconvenience caused if addresses have changed or sites have ceased to exist, but can accept no responsibility for any such changes.

A catalogue record for this book is available from the British Library.

A catalog record for this book is available from the Library of Congress.

	ISBN:	
	HB:	978-1-3504-1962-9
	PB:	978-1-3504-1961-2
	ePDF:	978-1-3504-1964-3
	eBook:	978-1-3504-1963-6

Series: Arden Performance Companions

Typeset by Integra Software Services Pvt. Ltd.
Printed and bound in Great Britain

For product safety related questions contact productsafety@bloomsbury.com.

To find out more about our authors and books visit www.bloomsbury.com and sign up for our newsletters.

'Shakespeare? He was a thief too.'

'The old works have their own values, their own differentiation, their own scale of beauty and truth. Those are what need to be uncovered.'

'To want the new is old-fashioned, what is new is to want the old.'

Bertolt Brecht

~

In memory of
Margot Heinemann (1913–92), Ralph Manheim
(1907–92) and John Willett (1917–2002)

CONTENTS

Series Preface xi

Introduction 1

Part One   Changing Worlds 9

    Bertolt Brecht (1898–1956) 11

Part Two   The Great Realist 21

1 Preparing 23
2 Rehearsing 61
3 Staging 91

Part Three   Six Plays 109

    Richard III 111
    As You Like It 125
    Measure for Measure 135
    King Lear 149
    Coriolanus 165
    The Tempest 177

Part Four   Questions and Suggestions 189

'He Made Suggestions' 191

Three Questions 193

Ten Suggestions 199

References 202
Index 207

SERIES PREFACE

The Arden Performance Companions offer practice-focused introductions to different aspects of staging Shakespeare's plays: whether accounts of how Shakespearean drama may respond to particular systems of rehearsal and preparation, guides to how today's actors can understand and use different facets of Shakespeare's verbal style, or explorations of how particular modern practitioners have used Shakespeare's scripts as starting points for their own embodied thinking about the social and aesthetic possibilities of popular theatre.

The premise of this series is that the interpretation of Shakespeare is not confined to the literary analysis of his scripts, but also includes their rehearsal and performance. With this in mind, the Arden list of editions of Shakespeare expanded in 2017 to include not only heavily-annotated scholarly texts of each play, designed primarily for use in colleges and universities, but a new series, the Arden Performance Editions of Shakespeare, designed primarily for use in rehearsal rooms and at drama schools. Just as academic editions of Shakespeare may be supplemented by books introducing students to different modes of academic criticism, so these Arden Performance Companions seek to supplement the Arden Performance Editions, offering a rich variety of practical guidance on how Shakespeare's plays can be brought to life in contemporary performance.

NOTE ON TEXTS

All quotations from Shakespeare are taken from the Arden Shakespeare Third Series, accessed through Drama Online.

Brecht Quotations

We are grateful to the Brecht Estate for permission to reproduce quotations from the following publications:

Berliner Ensemble Adaptations (2014), B. Brecht, eds. D. Barnett, J. Willett & T. Kuhn, trans. R. Manheim
Brecht: Diaries 1920–1922 (1979), trans. J. Willett, ed. H. Ramthun
Brecht: Journals 1934–1955 (1993), trans. H. Rorrison, ed. J. Willett
Brecht: Letters 1913–1956 (1990), trans. R. Manheim, ed. J. Willett
Brecht: Poems 1913–1956, (1976), eds. J. Willett & R. Manheim, trans. various
Brecht on Art and Politics (2003), eds. T. Kuhn & S. Giles
Brecht on Performance (2014), eds. T. Kuhn, S. Giles & M. Silberman
Brecht on Theatre (1964), trans. and ed. J. Willett
Brecht on Theatre (2015), eds. M. Silberman, S. Giles & T. Kuhn
Collected Plays, Volume Four (2001), B. Brecht, eds. T. Kuhn & J. Willett, trans. T. Kuhn
Collected Plays, Volume Six, Part Two (1981), B. Brecht, eds. J. Willett & R. Manheim, trans. R. Manheim

Introduction
The View from the Stalls

Directing Shakespeare Is Hard

Directing Shakespeare is hard and, as a grizzled veteran, I've often sat in the stalls watching a production in despair. But how should the young director go about it?

They might start by acknowledging the remoteness of Shakespeare's world. Whatever we may think of the many claims made for the playwright's 'universality', he wrote in a very different time, governed by alien attitudes and for an audience we would hardly recognize today. The plays follow literary and dramatic conventions which have almost completely disappeared and were first staged in a theatre whose social purpose could not be more alien. What's more, they have been subjected to so many re-evaluations, interpretations and performances in the four centuries since they were written that it's almost impossible to experience them with the open-minded attention that they deserve.

As a result, the young director may well wonder whether Shakespeare can be made to work today. This isn't just a matter of ghosts and fairies (although the rationalist *will* find such creatures problematic), it's the broader question of narrative credibility, especially the gender and class disguises, the episodes of all-consuming love at first sight and the apparently formulaic endings. And the characters are *peculiar*: the central figures often feel 'larger than life', with emotions disproportionate to the cause, while the smaller parts can seem irrelevant and are often laughed at or ignored.

The dramatic form can strike us as antique too, with a storytelling technique perplexing to an audience used to watching film and television. Directors and actors may admire the beauty of the language, while acknowledging that the syntax is antiquated, the verse dated and some of the language obscure. The text may express the character's thoughts and emotions, but there is little room for what in the modern theatre is called the 'subtext'. And while the young director may admire those passages of luminous humanity that we all gratefully stumble across, how should they read those scenes which suggest the opposite: hierarchy and sectarianism, nationalism and religious supremacy, snobbery and social division? Indeed, the young director shouldn't be blamed for feeling sceptical about whether Shakespeare belongs in our modern temples to inclusion, diversity and common decency.

And, finally, in putting the plays on stage, the director is confronted by some hard choices. How can they show the range of locations that the plays demand in such a way that the headlong flow of action isn't hindered, while also satisfying the modern audience's demand for visual stimuli? If they conclude that period costumes are off-putting, do they think jeans and t-shirts are any better? And if they plump for a modern setting, how can they represent the play's complex politics, let alone its enormous social range, when so many of the figures – not just servants and slaves but archbishops, princes and kings – are so unfamiliar? And last, but by no means least, how many actors can nail these extraordinary parts in all their emotional, political and intellectual complexity?

In trying to stage the plays today, then, the young director is confronted by a paradox: on the one hand, they know that the theatre must exist in the here and now; on the other, they understand that Shakespeare's plays often baffle modern audiences, especially those encountering them for the first time, and are often viewed through the filter of poor education, enforced reverence and received opinion. And so, staring glumly at actors struggling with alien language and an antique set of values, and surrounded by audiences not entirely sure what is unfolding in front of them, they may well be reminded that 'the past is a foreign country; they do things differently there'. And conclude, with a sigh, that it's perhaps not worth the trouble.

In brief, the young director must acknowledge the elephant in the room: If these plays come from an alien world, are written in an unfamiliar way and express such outdated values, why are we trying to stage them at all?

Schools of Directing

The eighty years since the Second World War have, seen a golden age in the performance of Shakespeare in Britain. The cobwebs of the Victorian and Edwardian stage have been blown away and modern audiences have been faced by a brave, if sometimes bewildering, new world in which pretty much anything is possible. Various approaches have been tried, often led by talented, industrious and influential directors, which can, for our purposes, be disentangled into four main schools.

The first is what is sometimes dubbed 'the Cambridge mafia'. Inspired by the literary critic FR Leavis and shaped by George ('Dadie') Rylands, the University of Cambridge's influential authority on Elizabethan theatre, its leading figures (all men) were Peter Hall, John Barton and Trevor Nunn. Their work at the RSC in the 1960s and 1970s combined close attention to the text with a robust sense of the dramatist engaged with the social issues of his day. Perhaps the most remarkable of their many triumphs was *The Wars of the* Roses (1963), an adaptation of the three parts of *Henry VI* and *Richard III*. Later members include the (almost all Cambridge-educated and again exclusively male) quintet of Richard Eyre, Nicholas Hytner, Sam Mendes, Gregory Doran and Dominic Dromgoole, whose productions have been seen at the RSC, the National Theatre, Shakespeare's Globe and the Bridge.

A second school emerged at the Royal Court Theatre in the 1960s, and was much influenced by Harley Granville Barker and the English naturalists. They pursued a more austere style, with the remarkable trio of John Dexter, William Gaskill and Peter Gill committed to what was sometimes dubbed 'poetic realism'. They introduced a new generation of largely working-class actors and championed an invigorated approach to performing, verse speaking and stage design. This cohort lacked the single-minded focus on Shakespeare that others pursued, preferring instead to set his plays alongside modern drama, treating the classics as new plays and new plays as classics. Nevertheless, they created some extraordinary productions at the Royal Court, the Riverside Studios and the National Theatre. Joan Littlewood at the Theatre Royal Stratford East could be described as an affiliate, as might the remarkable Howard Davies.

A more individualistic group took its inspiration from the great director Peter Brook, whose legendary productions of *King Lear* (1962) and *A Midsummer Night's Dream* (1970) at the RSC, and others at the Bouffes du Nord in Paris, set the highest possible bar. Taking his inspiration from the celebrated Polish critic Jan Kott, Brook insisted that Shakespeare should exist 'in the present tense' and did whatever he could to reimagine the great playwright as 'our contemporary'. His many followers include Buzz Goodbody, Adrian Noble, Michael Boyd, Deborah Warner, Declan Donnellan, Simon McBurney and Emma Rice, all of whom eschew (or eschewed) what Brook dubbed the 'deadly theatre' (Brook, 1968) in pursuit of something more theatrical, more immediate.

The last twenty years have seen the emergence of yet another group, who demand that the theatre should employ the enormous technical advance of recent years and subject Shakespeare to a ferociously sharp-edged and interventionist treatment. The key figures here are Ivo van Hove, Rupert Goold, Joe Hill-Gibbons, Robert Icke and the latest *wunderkind*, Rebecca Frecknall, with many others following in their wake.

The art of the theatre never stops evolving but all directors share the same view from the stalls. In their different ways, they all know that Shakespeare is hard, and want to find a way of staging it for the modern world. But how might we go about it?

Brecht and Me

These very different directors all take inspiration – often indirectly, sometimes slyly, usually unacknowledged – from the theatre of Bertolt Brecht: that extraordinarily prolific playwright, poet, director and theatrical provocateur who, first in pre-war Germany, then in exile in Scandinavia and America, and finally in the ruins of post-war East Berlin, insisted that drama should engage with the multiple disasters of his world. As Peter Brook declared, Brecht is 'the key figure of our time and all theatre work today at some point starts or returns to his statements and achievements' (Brook, 1968, 86). Certainly, the Berliner Ensemble's London seasons in the 1950s and 1960s had a galvanizing impact.

My own career has been modest in comparison, but in the last forty years I've directed twenty professional productions of Shakespeare and returned to four of the plays twice. I've tried most things, from radical filleting to academic austerity, period naturalism to modern dress, sometimes successfully, sometimes less so. As a result, but also from watching endless productions over the years, I've developed some doubts about whether these antique plays can *really* hold their own in the modern world. I also wonder whether some of the most hailed advances of recent years are also, in fact, steps backwards. But I am convinced that if we attend carefully to the details of the play in question, if we seek out the many conflicts and contradictions which are fundamental to its dramatic power, and if the actors bring a style of playing which is fresh, direct and connected, we stand the best chance of helping these remarkable works to live anew. It's not easy, but it must be possible.

Brecht is crucial to this sense of possibility. For the chief lesson I've taken from grappling with his influence over the years was the need to immerse myself in the strange world of Shakespeare's England even as I questioned and explored its enduring value. Brecht's example – as explained to me by some remarkable mentors – helped me look at the plays with a steady gaze and engage with them in a way that is intrigued and questioning, respectful and sceptical, ready to intervene but also prepared to stay silent: in theatre, I hope, as in life.

Brecht is an unfashionable figure today, often dismissed as dogmatic, the subject of frequently Germanophobic mockery more than intrigue, and one of the chief aims of this book is to celebrate the creative sophistication of his approach. Indeed, the Swiss director Benno Besson, often hailed as Brecht's natural successor, praised him for his 'attention to the world' and 'respect for everyone on stage' (Kleber and Visser, 1991, 115). And it is in the same spirit that Brecht's restless, pragmatic and dynamic view from the stalls offers, I believe, some of the most original, enjoyable and stimulating suggestions as to how we might stage Shakespeare today.

How to Use This Book

Understanding Brecht's approach to Shakespeare requires thinking as much as doing, reading as much as rehearsing, considering as much as coming to decisions. For Brecht's evolving practice was inspired by the evolving times in which he lived, and our understanding must be rooted in his understanding of those times. In other words, we can't stage Shakespeare's plays in a Brechtian fashion if we don't first *think* in a Brechtian fashion. And so, while my chief aim is to suggest ways that Brecht's example can help us stage Shakespeare today, I will also explore how he read the plays himself.

Part One places Brecht within his world and aims to show the way he engaged in the political, social and aesthetic questions of his time. Part Two scours Brecht's writings for his approach to his illustrious predecessor. In Part Three, I examine how Brecht's thinking might apply to six plays from across the canon, and in Part Four, I explore the three questions a Brecht-inspired director needs to ask when approaching a play by Shakespeare, and offer ten practical suggestions.

I regularly interrupt the narrative with what I call 'provocations, exercises and practical suggestions'. These allow the reader to step away from the historical and theoretical analysis and think about how to apply Brecht's ideas in the rehearsal room. These are necessarily exercises in thinking *and* exercises in practice, but I hope that together they will help clarify what Brecht was driving at, and help practitioners discover their own position in relation to his. While some will require thought and further reading, others demand improvisation and creativity. Some are tips for directing, others are suggestions for acting, but in their different ways they try to connect our work in the theatre with our understanding of the world beyond, in the way that Brecht would have wanted. Above all, they should be enjoyable.

The fact is, there are no clear answers to 'how to do Shakespeare as Brecht would have wanted', and this book doesn't pretend that there are. But I hope it will help actors and directors, students and teachers, think about a way of approaching Shakespeare which is informed by Brecht's reading of the plays and his practical work as a pioneering *homme du théâtre*. Above all, my aim is that it should help the reader sense afresh the dizzy-making and extraordinarily radical potential of the plays themselves.

Provocations, Exercises and Practical Suggestions

- Divide your group into two and ask half of them to list the things they find daunting about Shakespeare. Get them to do a short (quite possibly comic) presentation which explains the challenges that they face.
- Ask the other half of the group to do the same exercise describing all the things they find easy.
- Merge these two lists and create a brief dialogue which summarizes what your group feels about staging Shakespeare today. This could take the form of a dramatic conflict (and, again, could be comic).
- Even the youngest of the Shakespearean directors listed above was born in the last century: what might a fifth, distinctly twenty-first century school be called, and what qualities would it champion? Ask everyone to present a one sentence manifesto. For example: 'Shakespeare for Generation Y', 'Shakespeare for a Non-Binary World', 'Shakespeare and AI' and so on. If inspired, write a longer manifesto. Even develop a theory!
- Shakespeare's company didn't have stage directors and the role wasn't formulated until the nineteenth century. Divide your group into two and ask one group to rehearse a scene without a director and the other with one. What does a director offer? What are rehearsals like without one? Are directors necessary?

PART ONE

Changing Worlds

Bertolt Brecht (1898–1956)

Brecht was a voracious magpie, unashamed about the many influences on his work. These ranged from the masterpieces of German classical drama to American pulp fiction, the bracing challenges of Modernism to the austere restraint of the oriental theatre. He was exceptionally well-read, continuously productive and constantly questioning. Little, however, had as profound an impact on his work as the plays of William Shakespeare.

Brecht's views on Shakespeare kept evolving. This partly reflected his own creative development, but it was also a direct response to the many changes in the world in which he lived. He was suspicious of the idea that any work of art, however mighty, was universally relevant, and preferred to see how its resonances changed according to the changing times. And so we won't learn much about the way Brecht read Shakespeare if we don't first grasp something of the changing world in which he lived.

The Germany of Brecht's birth had been a united country for less than thirty years, and many of its leading politicians, artists and intellectuals were involved in an often-fractious debate about the identity of this loose federation of twenty-four city states. The exponential development of German industry, science and technology in the quarter century before the First World War, along with a dramatic growth in the urban proletariat and the expansion of her professional middle classes, is the essential background to Brecht's childhood and youth in Bavaria, and his emergence as a singular poetic voice.

Imperial Germany's experience of war and her surprise defeat in November 1918 swept this all aside, however, and the Weimar

Republic that appeared in its wake struggled to contain the hunger, poverty and runaway inflation that ensued. After the death of 2 million men and growing resentment at the punitive terms of the Versailles Treaty, Germany was a nation in crisis. The young Brecht saw at first hand the violent crushing of the Spartacist (Communist) revolution of January 1919 and his early, expressionist-influenced plays are as anguished as the society from which they sprang.

Remarkably, after four years of hyperinflation and mass unemployment, Germany's economy started to recover and she enjoyed five years of (relative) stability and a golden period of fine art, literature, music and theatre. Brecht moved to Berlin with his wife, the Austrian actress Helene Weigel in 1924, and these years saw his first successes (and controversies) as a playwright, polemicist and stage director, as well as the development of his ideas about what a progressive theatre might look like.

Weimar Germany's flowering was tragically short-lived, however, and over-dependent on American loans, her economy was devastated by the Wall Street Crash, triggering widespread unrest and political chaos. Indeed, the early 1930s saw pitched battles between communists and fascists, not just in parliament but on the streets. Artists and intellectuals were forced to take sides, and it was against this cataclysm that Brecht created his most explicitly political dramas. It was in this period, too, that he first read Karl Marx – himself a devoted Shakespearean – and started to clarify his views about what he called 'a theatre for the scientific age'.

With Hitler's rise to power, Brecht and his family were forced into exile. His books were burnt and there was little chance of his plays being performed in continental Europe, certainly not by professionals. Indeed, it is greatly to his credit that Brecht's six years as a refugee in Scandinavia were among his most productive, where he wrote a series of extraordinary plays reflecting the challenges of what he called the 'dark times', and studied classical drama with increasingly close attention.

In the summer of 1941 Brecht and his family crossed the Soviet Union and boarded a ship for Los Angeles. The cigar smoking, unwashed and frequently pugnacious Brecht was a fish out of water in wartime Hollywood, but it was there that he and many of the most significant German-speaking writers and artists debated the future of German culture, and it was overlooking the Pacific that he first glimpsed the Shakespearean-inspired grandeur of his mature theatrical vision. It was there, too, that he awaited the defeat of Nazi Germany and started to prepare for his return.

Brecht moved to Switzerland in late 1947, not returning to Berlin until October of the following year. In January 1949, he staged his legendary production of *Mother Courage and Her Children* in the bomb damaged Deutsches Theater and founded a theatre company, the Berliner Ensemble, which was eventually based at the Theater am Schiffbauerdamm, the site of his great Weimar triumph, *The Threepenny Opera*. With a core group of actors and other theatre artists from the pre-war left, supplemented by a new generation of young talent, Brecht set out to present a mixed repertoire of new plays (mostly by him) and revivals of the most progressive works of the classical repertoire.

Despite generous support from the newly founded East German state and growing international acclaim, Brecht in his final years was involved in continuous disagreements about cultural policy, especially about the classics, often with senior figures in the government. The struggle to create a progressive form of theatre continued.

Brecht and Shakespeare

British Shakespeareans sometimes underestimate the centrality of 'the Bard' to the German dramatic tradition. But the classical masterpieces of Johann Goethe, Friedrich Schiller and Heinrich von Kleist, and the more idiosyncratic works of Gotthold Ephraim Lessing, Jakob Lenz and Georg Büchner, all bear witness to his influence, with Shakespeare offering a mighty benchmark by which they could judge themselves and their rivals.

It's important to stress, however, that most of these playwrights – like Brecht himself – first encountered Shakespeare in German. Indeed, the translations of August Schlegel and Ludwig Tieck skilfully – subconsciously perhaps – reimagined Shakespeare as a German Romantic, and helped create the dominant view of him as the leading dramatist of a heroic elite, forging a new national identity. And it was with these translations that the notion of 'unser [our] Shakespeare' was born, so much so that Brecht once jokingly asked, 'Is Shakespeare English?' (Parker, 2014, 65). Shakespeare has been widely revived across Germany ever since, and we cannot assess Brecht's evolving views without taking this into account.

Evidence of Brecht's lifelong fascination with 'William the Great' (Kleber and Visser, 1991, 47) can be detected throughout his writings, from the early musings of the compulsive theatregoer in Bavaria to the careful articulations of the celebrated sage in his final years in Berlin. At his death, Brecht's library contained no less than sixty-three volumes of Shakespeare, in both English and German, and the number of references to Shakespeare in his collected works 'far outstrips those to Goethe or Schiller, Aristotle, even Marx' (Barnett, 2013, 113). Indeed, in Los Angeles at the height of the war, he was reading every night 'half a page of Shakespeare' (*J*, 1993, 327) and excitedly announced that the plays are 'extraordinarily full of life' (*BoP*, 2014, 89). Shakespeare was fundamental to the way that Brecht shaped his own work, and he took from him whatever he could.

Brecht was particularly drawn to Shakespeare's expressly political work: the history cycles, the problem plays, the Roman dramas and the mighty tragedies. Indeed, he described the histories as 'the closest to reality', explaining that 'there is no "idea" in them, no concern to shape a plot, scarcely any topicality': 'All you get', he announced excitedly, 'is an illumination of established facts with occasional corrections on the lines of "any other way is almost unthinkable"' (*J*, 1993, 167). Brecht's thinking can be profitably applied to the comedies and romances, but it was Shakespeare's 'darker purpose' (*King Lear*, 1.1.35) which attracted him most.

The Anglophone reader is fortunate that Brecht's plays have been extensively translated, edited and published. Many of them demonstrate Brecht's attempt to create a new kind of Shakespearean theatre for the modern world. His most significant theoretical essays and provocations appear in two indispensable volumes: *Brecht on Theatre* (1954, recently revised and expanded, 2015) and *Brecht in Performance* (2014). The somewhat overlooked *Brecht on Art and Politics* (2003) is a rewarding collection of essays, and the commentaries collected in his friend the great philosopher and aesthetician Walter Benjamin's *Understanding Brecht* (1998) are characteristically brilliant. Finally, Brecht's *Letters* (1990), *Diaries* (1979), *Poems* (1976) and *Journals* (1993) are all rich with Shakespearean insights.

Brecht's most sustained thinking on Shakespeare can be found in *The Messingkauf Dialogues* (1939–45), a remarkably fruitful collection of Socratic debates about the function of the theatre, largely written in exile in Scandinavia. They feature five imaginary speakers – a Philosopher, a Dramaturg, an Actor, an Actress and a Technician – and their contrasting views offer a typically dialectical approach to the art form. It's sometimes assumed that Brecht's own views are spoken by the Philosopher, or possibly the Dramaturg, but, as the editor Steve Giles insists, 'the notion that any of the characters might be Brecht's *raisonneur* is perverse' (*BoP*, 2014, 9), and it's more useful to see the ideas emerging in interaction with each other. Although the dialogues cover many subjects, there are several passages focusing on Shakespeare's theatre where, for the most part, the emphasis is on the difference between historical and contemporary practice, with fascinating suggestions into how understanding this can help us stage the plays today. I first encountered the *Messingkauf* in John Willett's bouncy translation (*MD*, 1965), which has been supplemented by a more scholarly (but perhaps less accessible) version in *Brecht on Performance* (2014, 1–125).

The other major commentary is the 'Short Organum for the Theatre'. Written in post-war Switzerland, this classically structured essay offers an orderly summary of Brecht's ideas about the performing arts, which, when they refer to Shakespeare, tend to celebrate the innate qualities of the writing. This, too, can be found in two translations: the first, by Willett, appears in the original edition of *Brecht on Theatre* (*BoT*, 1964, 179–204, 276–81); the revised translation is largely an improvement and is cited here (*BoT*, 2015, 271–308). Several of Brecht's other essays are illuminating, with perhaps the most rewarding being 'The Popular and the Realistic', 'Study of the First Scene of Shakespeare's *Coriolanus*' and 'Classical Status as an Inhibiting Factor' (*BoT*, 1964, 107–15, 252–65, 272–74).

Brecht's attempts to adapt Shakespeare's texts are mixed. His pre-war reworking of *Measure for Measure* as *Round Heads and Pointed Heads* (1936) is deeply flawed. Much better, I think, is his adaptation of *Coriolanus* (1952) which offers the clearest possible indication of the mature playwright's views. Brecht also collaborated on translations and adaptations of two of Shakespeare's contemporaries, notably his and Lion Feuchtwanger's successful take on Christopher Marlowe, *The Life of Edward II of England* (1924), and his less original adaptation with W. H. Auden of John Webster's *The Duchess of Malfi* (1944). He also wrote radio versions of *Macbeth* (1927) and *Hamlet* (1931), both sadly lost in the war, along with short exercise pieces for actors which draw on Shakespeare and Schiller (*BoP*, 2014, 127–41).

Brecht was drawn to scores of other English writers, whose empirical, earthy qualities offered a powerful contrast to the abstractions of the German tradition. The German playwright who had the greatest impact on Brecht's thinking was the early nineteenth-century young genius Georg Büchner, whose historical epic *Danton's Death* (1835) Brecht described as 'a superb melodrama': he knew that it lacked 'Shakespeare's roundedness', and was 'edgier, more intellectualised, more fragmentary, an ecstatic sequence of scenes' (*D*, 1979, 132), but it, along with the same writer's *Woyzeck* (1837), set the young Brecht on his route back to Shakespeare himself.

Brecht's views on Shakespeare's theatre were shaped by more than just 'high art' and he admired and borrowed from a vast range of popular artforms – the ballads and peepshows of the travelling fairs, the stern cadences of Luther's Bible and the hymns of the Salvation Army, the raucous comedy of the Bavarian comic Karl Valentin and the films of Charlie Chaplin, as well as detective stories, adventures and pulp fiction – all of which helped illuminate Shakespeare's own astonishingly popular and inclusive artform.

All this, along with a host of outstanding collaborators, interlocutors and opponents, helped shape one of the most idiosyncratic, dynamic and productive approaches to Shakespeare of modern times.

A Changing Approach

Brecht's interrogations of Shakespeare cannot be reduced to a simple formula. Indeed, as the great Marxist critic Margot Heinemann advises, 'It would be not merely pointless but distorting to try to construct a single closely coordinated, fully consistent argument out of all this rich material, whose multi-faceted fragmentary nature reflects Brecht's flexible, experimental approach' (1994, 228). We can, however, track a general shift in views.

The radical young playwright disliked the traditional German reverence for Shakespeare. Indeed, he declared in his twenties that it was 'futile to modernize or revise the classics, such as Shakespeare or the ancients', explaining that they are 'no longer workable [and] belong to another age' (Ewen, 1967, 162). He expressed a deeply held impatience with what he saw as Shakespeare's reactionary tendencies, most vividly caught in his quip that Shakespeare wrote 'drama for cannibals' (*BAP*, 2003, 70).

These old plays, he argued, should either be relegated to 'the dustbin of history' or subjected to a process of radical rewriting and alteration. It was, he thought, impossible to perform them 'just as they are' and any director who wanted to stage one of the plays should be expected to not just supply a radical interpretation of the existing text but shape, cut and alter it in such a way that its reactionary elements are exposed, and its progressive potential made visible. Indeed, he declared, 'one has to grapple with Shakespeare as one does with life' (Heinemann, 1994, 228).

Brecht never entirely renounced this impatience, but increasingly showed an appreciation of the complexity and sophistication of the original and came to admire the realism that shaped it. He understood that his mighty predecessor stood as a warning of how the classical tradition could be misappropriated, but also how it might still be useful. Thus, Shakespeare provided the mature Brecht with 'an exemplary type of theatre, alive with complexity, contradiction and historical realism', representing, as David Barnett puts it, 'the bar the Berliner Ensemble had to clear to prove itself a first-class theatre company' (Barnett, 2013, 126).

The *Observer*'s obituary hailed Brecht as 'the nearest equivalent to Shakespeare ever to appear anywhere', adding that 'if one believed in the transmigration of souls, one would be tempted to think he was Shakespeare reborn' (19 August 1956). Indeed, one could argue that not only did Shakespeare come to inspire Brecht's theatre more than any other but that Brecht's greatest achievement was writing Shakespearean drama for the modern world. And so, in studying the relationship between these two great dramatists, we will inevitably not just appreciate the light that Brecht cast on Shakespeare but also discover how his own achievements were inspired by his great predecessor's example.

Tracking this evolution from impatient rejection to meticulous negotiation lies at the heart of what follows. On the way we will encounter contradictions and dead ends, provocations and jokes, overstatements and innuendoes: such is the challenge in engaging with this slyest of theatre artists. Little in Brecht is straightforward, and navigating this mass of material will be challenging. But the quality of his insights deserves nothing less.

Other Brechtians

Of course, Brecht wasn't the first to be drawn to the political nature of Shakespearean drama and the observations of the great Romantic critics, especially William Hazlitt, frequently pre-empt Brecht's own. If the leading Victorian and Edwardian critics tended to underplay the plays' social content, especially the demystification of power that Brecht so admired, the mid-twentieth century saw several near contemporaries read Shakespeare in a way that he might have welcomed. Indeed, two seminal German language studies – Erich Auerbach's magisterial survey of European realism, *Mimesis* (1942–5) and Robert Weimann's *Shakespeare and the Popular Tradition* (1978) – echo Brecht's work in crucially important ways.

A handful of modern critics have engaged in parallel lines of inquiry, including Chris Fitter, Richard Wilson, Kiernan Ryan, William Carroll and Annabel Paterson. But commentators and practitioners often overlook Shakespeare's exploration of wealth, power and labour in favour of other identity issues, especially gender, race and sexuality, and Brecht's own thoughts about Shakespeare have been largely ignored. Brecht's biographers have alluded to the subject, as have writers on his theatrical practice, but it is striking that for all the studies of Brecht's theatre, let alone the hundreds of volumes of Shakespearean criticism, this is the first book-length study in English of the subject.

There are, fortunately, two very good essays, both of which I cite extensively: 'Brecht as Great Shakespearean' (2013) by David Barnett is a scholarly study which covers the main points admirably, while Margot Heinemann's 'How Brecht Read Shakespeare' (1994) is an older, more discursive piece by one of the legendary figures of the British left. The two are interestingly complementary: where the first analyses Brecht's approach in historical detail, the second is informed by generational understanding and a life dedicated to social justice.

Indeed, it was Margot Heinemann who introduced me to the subject as an undergraduate, and if anyone is the inspiration for what follows, it is this remarkable woman. The others are the original co-editors of the English Brecht: John Willett, who did so much to introduce Brecht to Britain, and the much-loved translator Ralph Manheim. I was lucky as a young man to have had these three as my mentors, and I remember sitting with Margot and John in a pub in Hampstead, discussing the need for such a book. I flatter myself that they would have approved.

Provocations, Exercises and Practical Suggestions

- This first exercise is deliberately frivolous: ask your group to imagine ten Shakespearean directors for each of the decades of the last 100 years and get them to explain their approach: an elegant Noel Coward-like dandy in the 1920s, a ferocious Communist intellectual of the 1930s, a patriotic wartime Englishman in the 1940s, a 1950s existentialist, a long-haired 1960s hippy, a 1980s feminist, a free market Thatcherite of the 1980s, a concerned internationalist of the 1990s, a traumatized globalist of the 2000s, a populist of the 2010s and so on. The result will be thick with caricature but could perhaps illuminate how attitudes to Shakespeare have changed, and continue to change.

- Write a simple chronology of the main features of Brecht's life in one column and set it against a chronology of the world in which he lived. A model for this can be found in my *Guide to the Plays of Bertolt Brecht* (Unwin, 2005, 249–58). Then consider Brecht's relationship to the historical events of his time and explore how he responded: an isolated, if celebrated, voice in Weimar Germany; persecuted by the Nazis and hated by Stalin during the 1930s and 1940s: mocked and rejected in wartime Hollywood; and supported but continually criticized by the new regime in post-war Berlin.

- Ask your group to improvise a short scene which imagines a modern theatre director from sub-Saharan Africa or the Middle East arriving in Britain, speaking no English and being interviewed for a production by a well-established British Shakespearean. What might the points of connection be, but what are the differences? Explore, for example, how both figures might say that Shakespeare is 'universal' but have quite different notions of what such 'universality' means. This would help the group see the way different cultural backgrounds shape different attitudes, and that we should be careful before we assume the existence of shared values.

PART TWO

The Great Realist

1

Preparing

Working in the Brechtian circle of attention requires careful thought. Indeed, I suggest, you cannot make theatre in a Brechtian fashion if you don't first think in a Brechtian fashion.

If some of what follows seems to belong outside of the rehearsal room, it's because theory and practice, art and politics, thinking and doing have rarely been so closely allied. Brecht wasn't just a remarkable playwright and director, he was also a significant cultural, political and philosophical thinker in his own right. It is my hope that by engaging with this preparatory material the reader will be able to grasp the intimate, and constantly evolving relationship between the theatre and the world beyond the stage door which was so central to Brecht's approach to Shakespeare.

Why Theory?

'A man with one theory is lost', the young Brecht joked, 'He must have several, four, lots! He should stuff them in his pockets like newspapers, hot from the press' (Parker, 2014, 155). The unwary, however, are often baffled and ask plaintively, 'Why do we need all this? Surely the work should speak for itself?'

In wrestling with this, directors would do well to consider what is meant by 'theatrical theory'. They should start by considering the German tradition of 'dramaturgy', exemplified in Gotthold Ephraim Lessing's *Hamburg Dramaturgy* (1767), an extraordinarily influential collection of over a hundred short essays on drama and theatre, including several on Shakespeare. And even today, every self-respecting German theatre has its 'dramaturgs', resident intellectuals who produce critical analyses of the playtext, explaining the conceptual framing of the production and offering audiences insights into what they are watching.

Brecht's dramaturgical writings belong to this tradition, but are, for the most part, more practical in orientation. Brecht knew that his own stubbornly difficult plays could be easily misinterpreted and was keen to ensure that directors and actors understood what he was getting at in terms of not just form but content too. What's more, despite the occasional obscurity of his theoretical style (sometimes compounded by awkward translation), Brecht knew that clarity was essential; indeed, he kept in his study a little wooden donkey with a sign hanging around its neck declaring, 'Even I must be able to understand it' (Benjamin, 1998, 108).

Consequently, the word 'theory', with its association of airy abstraction, is perhaps misleading with Brecht, that most empirical of thinkers. Indeed, late in life, when pressed about why so many hostile responses to his theatre 'give no account of what it is really like', he was disarmingly candid:

> My own fault ... My whole theory is much naïver than people think, or than my way of putting it allows them to suppose.
> (*BoT*, 1964, 247–8)

The fact is, Brecht adjusted his ideas to fit the new realities, and much of his theory is simply an articulation of what he was already doing in practice.

Provocations, Exercises and Practical Suggestions

- List as many late nineteenth- and twentieth-century theoretical approaches to the theatre as you can: Stanislavski, Meisner, Artaud, Meyerhold, Piscator, Lee Strasberg, Uta Hagen, Grotowski, Brook, Hall, Lecoq and so on. Try to distil into a couple of sentences what each one stood for. Then, as you work through this book, see where their ideas overlap with Brecht's, but also where they differ.

- Harder, but do the same with earlier theorists: Aristotle, Horace, Boileau, Diderot, Lessing, Freytag, Zola and others. Above all, try to understand what Brecht was reacting against.
- Discover whatever you can about Shakespeare production in Germany before Hitler, both traditional and radical, and share as many images and accounts as you can find. This is the aesthetic context for Brecht's innovations.

Politics and the Theatre

Brecht was, above all, a political dramatist, eager to show the way that the world works and challenge the injustice that is its regular consequence. 'The modern theatre', he wrote:

> Needs to be questioned not about its degree of conformity with the 'eternal laws of the theatre' but about its ability to master the rules governing the great social processes of our age; not about whether it manages to interest the spectator in buying a ticket… but about whether it manages to interest him in the world.
>
> (*BoT*, 1964, 161)

Indeed, Brecht's underlying aim was to encourage the audience to become 'curious, questioning, and active member[s] of society' (2015, 24).

Brecht's political aspiration was, above all, Marxist: 'The theatre has hitherto interpreted the world', he insisted (adapting a famous phrase from Marx), 'the point is to change it'. Indeed, he confessed that 'when I read Marx's *Capital*, I understood my plays' (*BoT*, 1964, 23n), and the same can be said of his reading of Shakespeare. While his aim, he insisted, was 'less to moralize than to observe', the 'thick end of the wedge followed: the story's moral'.

Politics, however, are complicated, and Brecht's critics point to those times when he seemed ambivalent or, worse, backed the authorities against ordinary people. In his defence, we should remember that Brecht was one of the leading cultural figures in the opposition to Hitler and that he and his family fled Berlin in fear for their lives; indeed, his work consistently condemned fascism in the strongest terms imaginable and he largely eschewed the binary choices of the

Cold War. Above all, he wanted his audiences to be 'entertained with the wisdom that comes from the solution of problems, with the anger that is a practical expression of sympathy with the underdog, with the respect due to those who respect humanity' (*BoT*, 1964, 186). It's hardly a call for revolutionary violence.

'Alter the world, it needs it!' sings the Chorus in *The Decision* (*CP*, 1997, 79), however, and Brecht understood that while kindness and decency has its value, it alone cannot prevent injustice. Indeed, Brecht showed, goodness is often deployed to protect the interests of the powerful. We can certainly agree that fascism needed more than kind words if it was to be defeated, as the communists and socialists who were the first to take arms against it in the 1930s demonstrated so bravely. As a result, those of us 'born later' should surely, as Brecht implored, 'Remember / When you speak of our failings / The dark times too / Which you have escaped' (*P*, 1976, 319).

The relationship of all this to Shakespearean drama is complex, to put it mildly. But just as Brecht realized that the process of historical change is messy, so he understood that Shakespeare portrays the complex realities of a changing world, free of simplistic notions of right and wrong, progressive and reactionary, good and bad. Indeed, Shakespeare brings us face to face with the contradictory stuff of history: thick with conflict and often bloody, but always, eventually, bringing about change. And it's here that Brecht's engagement with Shakespeare as a political dramatist can be found.

Provocations, Exercises and Practical Suggestions

- Improvise two short dramatic scenes: the first consists of two politicians talking to each other about their summer holidays; the second has two lorry drivers talking about their work. Which is the more 'political'? And why? In other words, do politicians only talk about politics, and are ordinary people apolitical?
- List some of the causes of injustices in the world that you feel most passionately about: racism, inequality of opportunity, ableism, snobbery, poverty, the climate crisis, ethno-nationalism and so on. Then check this against your knowledge of Shakespeare and see whether he supports

what you believe in or reinforces what you detest. But also the extent to which he appears entirely ignorant of either. Keep this list to hand as you work through this book.

'Documents in Barbarism'

To engage fully with the classics of the past, Brecht knew, required a hefty dollop of scepticism. This was best expressed by his friend the philosopher Walter Benjamin, who, in a famous passage, insisted that the great works of the past should be viewed with 'cautious detachment', arguing that 'there is no document of civilization which is not at the same time a document of barbarism' (Benjamin, 1970, 258).

Likewise, the modern director of Shakespeare should be alert to the values that the plays apparently promote, whether vicious ones like snobbery, racism, nationalism, ableism and sexism, or more conventionally virtuous ones such as romantic love, religious devotion, social responsibility, hard work and independence of mind. To what extent, Brecht asks, do the old plays champion an ideology that furthers the oppression of minorities, denies human rights and increases inequality? Are they an embodiment of the progressive's dreams or something darker and less appealing?

The answer is complex and Brecht dismissed the tone of this debate as 'terrifyingly unproductive' (*J*, 1993, 304):

> A dialectician would find no difficulty in the dispute about whether the great bourgeois writers represent humanity or the bourgeoisie, since they were members both of mankind and of the bourgeoise at the same time, and thus contradictory beings. They represent mankind as members of the bourgeoisie and the bourgeoisie as members of humanity in general.
>
> (*J*, 1993, 305)

Indeed, whether Shakespeare's *Complete Works*, often hailed as a supremely valuable 'document of civilization', should *also* be regarded as a 'document of barbarism' is a key question for anyone approaching the plays today.

Such wrestling with the cultural inheritance landed Brecht in trouble, not just in Weimar Germany and 1940s Hollywood, but post-war East Germany too. For while the new regime welcomed the fame that Brecht brought, they found his habitual questioning of the classical inheritance a challenge. Indeed, he was publicly 'criticised for having the audacity to apply his theories to the performances of Shakespeare and not limiting them to his own plays'. It was even said that his denial of national traditions was 'alien to the people' (Barnett, 2015b, 92–3).

At the heart of such objections was the accusation of 'formalism', the Stalinist sin of prioritizing artistic form over representing 'the people'. Although modern commentators scoff at such talk, Brecht was more nuanced. He recognized the role of culture in building a better society after the horrors of the Third Reich and knew that it should take inspiration from working people themselves. But he turned the argument back on his critics and argued that they were taking their inspiration from other works of art, not everyday life (*BoT*, 1964, 112). In other words, they were the real 'formalists'.

Brecht wanted theatre artists to develop, above all, a degree of critical objectivity: 'We have to see the work afresh', he insisted, 'we cannot go on looking at it in the degenerate, routine-bound way common to the theatre of a degenerating bourgeoisie' (*BoT*, 1964, 272). The underlying problem, he insisted, was a 'mistaken conception of the work's classical status':

> If we allow ourselves to be inhibited by a fake, superficial, decadent, petty bourgeois idea of what constitutes a classic then we shall never achieve lively and human performances.
> (*BoT*, 1964, 273)

In other words, we need to make up our own mind about Shakespeare's enduring value and not take it for granted. And this is central to everything that follows.

Provocations, Exercises and Practical Suggestions

- Ask the members of your group to share their first encounter with Shakespeare. Get them to act out (satirically, if they like) what they were told. Discuss what young people should learn about Shakespeare instead.

- Discuss your favourite Shakespeare play and identify three elements that, in your opinion, qualify it as a 'document in barbarism'.
- Do the same and identify three elements that qualify it as 'a document in civilization'.
- Divide your group into two and dramatize a debate between the two positions. Ensure that both are equipped with the best arguments you can find.

Reading Shakespeare Historically

Ben Jonson declared that Shakespeare's work was 'not of an age, but for all time'. Brecht would have replied that Shakespeare's age was very different to our own and that this eulogy should be read sceptically. Or rather, that Jonson's praise of his friend as the 'soul of the age' was more to the point.

Brecht's understanding of history was shaped, above all, by the nineteenth-century German philosopher, G.W.F. Hegel, who argued that in human affairs a 'thesis' comes into conflict with an 'antithesis', which eventually produces a 'synthesis', which in turn offers a further 'thesis', *ad infinitum*. This interactive dance, Hegel claimed, was the engine of progress, and the clashes between individuals, classes and groups shaped the world. Such 'dialectical materialism', Brecht explained, 'regards nothing as existing except in so far as it changes' (*BoT*, 1964, 193).

Turning to Shakespeare's England, Marxists like Brecht rejected the notion of a stable nation state with a fixed hierarchy, and stressed, instead, a time of momentous upheaval. They traced the decline of the old nobility and the emergence of the gentry, the shift from centuries of unchallenged Catholicism to the brave new world of the Protestant Reformation, along with a growing questioning of monarchical powers and the emergence of new democratic thinking. They observed how the universalist communities of the medieval world gave way to individualism and competition, and led within a generation to civil war and the execution of the king. They insisted that England was a country in crisis, where the contours of the past were being reinterpreted, just as the shapes of the future were being created: a challenging time to be alive, no doubt, but tremendously fertile territory for the great dramatist.

In studying Brecht's reading of Shakespeare, this emphasis on constant change is fundamental. Thus, in reading *Henry V* we should observe the way a special bond between monarch and the people was increasingly being deployed in Elizabethan England as a way of countering aristocratic ambition, while the old myth of the 'divine right of kings' was both reasserted and challenged. Similarly, in considering Hamlet's characteristic 'hesitancy', we should explore the intellectual and cultural formation that makes him (at least temporarily) 'hesitant': only a prince, we might note, has the leisure to indulge in such introspection, and Hamlet's education in Wittenberg, the crucible of Protestantism, offers him a perfect template for the new individualistic attitude to duty and conscience that shapes his behaviour. In other words, Hamlet's 'hesitancy' is symptomatic of the intellectual fashion of his time, and not simply a quirk of his character. Entire belief systems were changing and good plays capture a world in flux.

Such a dynamic view of history begs an important philosophical question. For if, as conservatives insist, human nature is always the same, the challenges faced by people in the past will have been the same as ours. The Marxist, by contrast, argues that people are shaped by the society in which they live, which is continuously evolving:

> If we ensure that our characters on the stage are moved by social impulses and that these differ according to the period, then we make it harder for our spectator to identify himself with them. He cannot simply feel: that's how I would act, but at most can say: if I had lived under those circumstances.
>
> (*BoT*, 1964, 190)

Thus, it is only by grasping the fundamental strangeness of Shakespeare's world, Brecht argued, that we can understand the belief systems that shape his characters and the choices that they make.

Brecht insisted that it was dangerous to generalize about historical conditions from individual incidents:

> Historical incidents are unique transitory incidents associated with particular periods. The conduct of the persons involved in them is not fixed and 'universally human'; it includes elements that have been or may be overtaken in the course of history and is subject to criticism from the immediately following period's point of view.
>
> (*BoT*, 1964, 140)

In other words, historical context cannot be simplified: it is embodied in individuals and their particular position, and the nature of the time is the sum of such responses. Drama with all its capacity for contradiction and representation of individual experience is the ideal artistic form to show a world in flux.

In the process, Brecht savaged the 'miserable philistine's' view that his experiences are identical to those of Shakespeare's 'heroes':

> Anything can happen to him, he's at home in any disaster. He's been rewarded with ingratitude like Lear, he's raged like Richard III, he's given up just about everything for his wife, as Antony did for Cleopatra, and hectored her more or less as Othello did his, he is as hesitant as Hamlet to right a wrong by shedding blood, and his friends are like Timon's. He is exactly like everybody, and everybody is like him. Differences don't matter to him, to him it's all the same.
>
> (*BoP*, 2014, 56)

Instead, a historical reading of Shakespeare will require us to use our historical imagination and engage with historical difference and change.

The environment in which the plays were produced is alien too. Thus we should remember the 'brute and bloodstained fact of state censorship' (Fitter, 2012, 431) under which Shakespeare wrote: all sorts of subjects were forbidden (the representation of living people and most discussions of theology, for a start) and playwrights had to be careful not to offend their masters. As a result, we have to listen to what is *not* said along with what is said, and this will require our historical imagination. This is doubly important with those characters who risk life, limb and livelihood for speaking truth to power, but it is here that the forces of change are often to be found.

Plays aren't historical documentaries, however, and we don't have to be historians to work with a historical perspective:

> The pleasure given by representations of such different sorts hardly ever depended on the representation's likeness to the thing represented. Incorrectness, or considerable improbability even, was hardly or not at all disturbing, so long as the correctness had a certain consistency and the improbability remained of a constant kind.
>
> (*BoT*, 1964, 182)

What matters is to see the plays as offering stories of social and political change, and deploy our imagination, knowledge and life experience in bringing them to the stage. Embracing this creative tension between past and present, stasis and change, history and modernity, individuality and the mass is the important point.

Provocations, Exercises and Practical Suggestions

- Shakespeare, Brecht always insisted, lived in a rapidly changing world. Ask each member of your group to summarize some of the conflicting perspectives of the time: 'God is everything', 'God doesn't exist'; 'My loyalty is to the Pope', 'My loyalty is to the Queen'; 'Poor people need help', 'Poor people have only themselves to blame' and so on. See how many contradictory positions you can discover.
- Divide your group into pairs (as close as possible in terms of gender, age, class, race) and ask them to improvise a scene between a young person today and the same (biological) person in 1600. Let today's person explain what it is like living in the modern world (mobile phones, feminism, human rights, multiculturalism, post-imperialism, climate change etc.) and let the person from 1600 be amazed and, perhaps, appalled.
- Ask your group to do the same in reverse. This will help them discover just how much has changed in the last 400 years.

Playing Shakespeare Historically

Brecht didn't just expect us to read Shakespeare's plays historically, he wanted us to perform them with historical understanding. But how do we do this in the theatre, that most transient of art forms, with an audience whose historical knowledge is inevitably limited?

Some argue loudly that we should just be 'true to the period'. But the Brechtian treats all attempts at reconstruction with caution: it's impossible to know how the plays were originally staged, let alone the way the actors performed or interacted with their audience, and period costumes (insofar as we can understand them) can have all sorts of unintended consequences. Strict 'authenticity' is a dead end.

The opposite has its dangers, too, however: namely, imagining that modern life offers direct parallels to Shakespeare's time and place. We see this in productions which dress everyone in business suits, surrounded by chic furniture: it is as if Shakespeare were writing about the North London intelligentsia, not Early Modern England. As Brecht wrote:

> When our theatres perform plays of other periods they like to annihilate distance, fill in the gap, gloss over the differences. But what becomes then of our delight in comparisons, in distance, dissimilarity – which is at the same time a delight in what is close and proper to ourselves.
>
> (*BoT*, 1964, 276)

By exploring the play as a historical phenomenon, rich with conflict and change, a space opens up which helps us notice its enduring relevance: as Brecht put it, directors and designers should 'leave [the plays] their distinguishing marks and keep their impermanence always before our eyes, so that our own period can be seen to be impermanent too' (*BoT*, 1964, 190).

It's important to recognize that the choice of setting has an impact on the play's meaning. Thus, *Twelfth Night*, even with the full text unchanged, is very particular if set in Mussolini's Italy; likewise, *The Taming of the Shrew* remains intriguing if the action unfolds in a culture that hasn't yet embraced feminism. Different settings, if taken seriously, affect the play in different ways – its rhythms and emphases, as much as its actions and meanings – and directors need to calculate the consequences of their decisions carefully. Again, thought is required.

Brecht expected us to do two things at once: understand Shakespeare's plays as the products of their time, even as we plumb them for contemporary resonance. The important thing is seeing them in contrast with today: 'It is only against the background of our time that [the plays'] form emerges as an old form, and without this background I doubt they would have any form at all' (*BoP*, 2014, 92). The result – what I sometimes call 'theatrical bifocalism' – is suggested in a key passage in *The Messingkauf Dialogues*:

> We too are the parents of a new age, but the children of an old one; we understand a lot about the remote past, and we are still able to share emotions that were once overwhelming and aroused on a grand scale. And the society we live in is just as complex, too ... All the same, there is much in these works that is dead, distorted and empty. It can stay in the books, because we can't tell whether it's really dead or only seems to be, and because it may help explain other phenomena of that bygone age. I'd almost prefer to draw your attention to the wealth of living elements to be found in these works at seemingly dead points. A tiny addition and they spring to life, now of all times, and for the first time.
>
> (*BoP*, 2014, 92)

Stumbling across such 'living elements' is one of the chief pleasures in working on Shakespeare. The challenge is that they often sit alongside the opposite: material which is 'dead, distorted and empty'. Brecht wants us to engage with both.

Thus, performing Shakespeare historically is a complex business. We need to reject both 'historicism' (the aesthetic commitment to the surface of life in the past) and 'contemporaneity' (the simple substituting of old settings for modern ones), and show instead how the historic conflicts of Shakespeare's time are embodied in the action, but can be understood today. What is required is nothing less than the development of an entirely modern way of presenting the dynamic dramas of history. This, as we'll see, is the central outcome of following Brecht's example.

Provocations, Exercises and Practical Suggestions

- Devise a short play with two people: one who is wealthy, the other who is poor. Explore how many different factors contribute to their relative status and see how a further definition (age, skin colour, health, employment status etc.) changes the drama further.
- Whichever time period you chose for your scene, now choose a different time period (at least twenty-five years remote from the original) and re-improvise the scene, noting how everything feels different.
- Discuss two approaches to staging Shakespeare today: one using historical costumes, the other using modern ones. Describe the strengths and weaknesses of each and discover which you prefer. And now describe the limitations of your preferred approach.
- Take an episode from Shakespeare where a powerful person is talking to a less powerful one. Two examples might be: Cleopatra's questioning of the messenger who brings the news of Antony's marriage to Octavia (*Antony and Cleopatra*, 2.5.23–106) or Macbeth's briefing of the two men he employs to murder Banquo and his son Fleance (*Macbeth*, 3.1.73–139). Ask the actors to play the scene twice, in two different contexts: one in Shakespeare's time and the other today. Remind the actors in the modern version of some simple facts: universal suffrage, comprehensive education, employment rights, health and safety regulation, the welfare state, equal rights and so on, and see how that affects the scene (or indeed makes it unplayable). And then, when they play it historically, remind them of the absence of all these rights and protections, and see how the action changes accordingly.

Three Approaches

The modern British theatre offers three main approaches to staging Shakespeare. All are related to Brecht, but deserve to be disentangled.

The first is the attempt to make the plays speak to a modern audience directly. This was robustly articulated in Jan Kott's *Shakespeare Our Contemporary* (1964), a seminal work of modern criticism, most brilliantly realized on stage in the work of the director Peter Brook. But while Brecht would have enjoyed Kott's energy and admired Brook's verve, it's hard to imagine him embracing their conclusions. Brecht dismissed existentialism as the philosophy of the disaffected intellectual and would have found Kott's pessimism hard to swallow. He would also have dismissed Kott's view of Shakespeare's history plays as merely mechanistic, leaving no space for critical thought. But the biggest stumbling block for Brecht is that the pursuit of absolute contemporaneity too readily denies the fact of historical change.

The second approach is to proclaim Shakespeare's universality. This reads the plays as dramatizations of mythical archetypes and ignores anything which locates them in their time and place. The aim is to discover the deep roots of the stories and allow them to work on the subconscious. Again, Brecht would have found this concerning: not only was he suspicious of the substitution of myth for an engagement with concrete reality, such mythopoeia had provided the cultural background to German fascism. What's more, if drama is to be stripped of its historical and geographical coordinates, Brecht knew, its social content disappears. Thus, if Shakespeare is asked to mean everything to everyone, he quickly doesn't mean anything to anyone. Consequently, what Peter Brook dismissed as the 'permissive attitude' towards Shakespeare production is sadly widespread (Berry, 1977, 124).

The third approach is to locate the plays in a society remote from Shakespeare's own and embrace the energies that it releases. Thus, *Measure for Measure* is set in Freud's Vienna, *The Merchant of Venice* relocated to Las Vegas and *As You Like It* plays out in a holiday camp in Bridlington. Thousands of such translocations have been attempted, occasionally offering insights, but are all too often merely capricious. The problem is that the audience's primary engagement is with the setting and not with the drama itself. It often makes for pleasurable theatre, but doesn't reveal much about the play.

Brecht's estimation of Shakespeare's worth didn't depend on discovering fortuitously similar experiences, nor in rendering the world of his plays in an abstract form, let alone offering a random historical parallel. Rather, he wanted us to scour them for the way that they expose the contradictions of his time and dramatize the conflicts which bring about change. The forces involved can be progressive or reactionary, or both simultaneously, and the struggles can be between all kinds of individuals, classes and groups, but the critical point is that they are played out on the stage and made evident to the audience. Thus, Shakespeare's plays, according to Brecht, are nothing less than dialectics in practice.

Provocations, Exercises and Practical Suggestions

- Consider these three different approaches with reference to your favourite Shakespeare play. Imagine what each production might be like. Describe each one's strengths and weaknesses, and decide which you prefer. What would be sacrificed by these different approaches, and what would be gained?

Realism

Central to Brecht's work in the theatre was the much-contested notion of 'realism'. Most great writers have their own understanding of this term, and Brecht was no exception. But students mesmerized by Brechtian artifice may be surprised by his commitment to what is often assumed to be its opposite.

Realism should be differentiated from naturalism, best understood as an artistic genre developed in the late nineteenth century which insisted that the stuff of everyday life – railway stations, divorce courts, bank accounts and so on – are legitimate subjects for art. Such a view is certainly valuable, as the novelist Émile Zola insisted in his *Naturalism in the Theatre* (1881): 'There is more poetry in the little apartment of a bourgeois than in all the empty, worm-eaten palaces of history.' But this is not the same as Brecht's realism, an artistic method which rejected both the abstractions of idealism and the limitations of naturalism, and explored, instead, the way that human life is shaped by the realities of class and power, wealth and status, and undergoes change and upheaval as a result. Naturalism is not antithetical to Brecht, but realism is the more useful concept.

The audience, Brecht argued, will learn little about how capitalism works by putting a working factory on stage; instead, he should be shown who operates its machines, who pays for them and what happens to their profits. Similarly, Brecht insisted, Shakespeare didn't write 'realistically' that things have always been as they are, he shows that they can 'realistically' change and continue to change. It's a provocative and highly political view of realism, aligning artistic production with the processes of history itself. It draws on the materialism of naturalism, but casts it in a new and radical light.

Brecht's most penetrating insights into realism can be found in an essential passage in *The Messingkauf Dialogues*, where the Philosopher responds testily to a question from the Actor about the danger of 'inconsistencies':

> The old chronicles are full of such things. It's impossible to perform these medieval plays anyway to spectators who have no sense of history. It would be a stupid thing to do. But Shakespeare is a great realist, and I think he would stand the test. He always shovelled a lot of raw material on to the stage, unvarnished representations of things he has seen.
>
> (*BoP*, 2014, 92)

The matter is explored further when the Philosopher is questioned about whether actors and directors should be 'bound hand and feet by the playwright's text'. In response, he describes the dynamic role of these lumps of 'raw material', which offer so much more than mere history:

> You could treat the text as a report which is authentic but has several meanings. A vaguely defined Caesar, so you are told, finding himself surrounded by aristocratic assassins, murmured to a certain Brutus 'Et tu, Brute'. A report like that, if it comes not from a line in a play but from some other source, does not tell its hearers very much, their knowledge of the world is not significantly increased. Even if they are inclined to generalize, they can do so in a whole number of false directions. Then you, the actor, burst into this vague, nebulous conception and

represent life itself. By the time you've finished, your spectators should have seen more than even an eyewitness of the original incident would have.

(*BoP*, 2014, 49–50)

The central point is that the work of the 'great realist' is rooted in everyday life and the theatre should embrace the fact: 'Shakespeare couldn't have written just for his desk drawer, any more than I can', Brecht wrote. 'Besides, he had his characters before his eyes. The people he depicted were running around in the streets. He just observed their behaviour and picked out a few traits; there were many others, just as important, that he left out' (Jameson, 1977, 105–6). Indeed, Brecht's Shakespeare, David Barnett explains, had a 'materialist grasp of reality *avant la lettre*' (2013, 116): 'The audience should see not simply people who do their own deeds ... but human beings, shifting raw material, uniform and undefined, that can surprise them' (Heinemann, 1994, 80).

It is this materialist understanding of the complexities and contradictions of human life that produces the rich realism that Brecht strove for, and which he found so manifestly in Shakespeare, where individuals are *both* members of a group and granted individual agency, reflecting their own interests and interpreting them in individual ways. For it is only by discovering what very different individuals have in common that we can understand what defines the group. Thus, not every aristocrat in Shakespeare is contemptuous of those who work for him, though many are; not every king champions the notion of divine right, although some do; and while many working people look forward to a better world in the future, others look back to a golden age in the past. Such contradictions are more than mere hypocrisy: they reveal the range of positions that the individual takes in response to a particular set of class-defined conditions and it is unrealistic to imagine anything else. After all, as Brecht gleefully insisted, 'You are not portraying principles, but human beings' (*BoP*, 2014, 76).

And so, the actor playing Williams in *Henry V* should understand that he combines traditional loyalty to the king with modern scepticism about the idea that men like him should lay down their lives in his service. Similarly, an actor performing Jack Cade in

Henry VI Part Two should recognize the same mixture of righteous anger and appalling self-indulgence, visionary dreams of the future and yearnings for a lost world, savage cruelty and rare egalitarian manners that can be detected in our own populist politicians today. It's not that the characters have direct modern equivalents, it's that in their historical contradictions modern contradictions can be glimpsed. Thus, as Brecht maintained, observations of everyday life are 'a major part of acting' (*BoT*, 1964, 196).

Brecht's notion of realism is explored further in *Aesthetics and Politics* (1977), an essential volume of essays by the leading figures of the so-called Frankfurt School. Perhaps the most significant for our purposes is Brecht's response to the Hungarian Marxist critic György Lukács' argument that only writers working within the traditions of the nineteenth-century novel can claim to be realistic. Brecht turned this on its head and celebrated, instead, the full range of literary techniques. 'Realism is not a mere question of form', he insisted: 'Were we to copy the style of the realists, we would no longer be realists' (Jameson, 1977, 86). It is revealing to then read Lukács eulogize Brecht posthumously as 'the greatest realist playwright of his age', largely, it seems, because of what he took from Shakespeare (Lukács, 1963, 89). Indeed, Brecht understood that Shakespeare's realism flourished in the entirely anti-naturalistic conditions of the Elizabethan stage.

Erich Auerbach's *Mimesis* (1946) goes further. This offers three key insights into the development of European realism. The first is that the great poets of the Italian Renaissance rejected the conventional hierarchies of their times and, by including all classes, achieved striking three-dimensionality in their effects. Second, that writing that denies the lower classes their own viewpoint cannot be deemed realistic and Auerbach dismisses anything that merely privileges the ruling elite as idealist. Finally, that the greatest writers employ the vernacular liberally. All three can be usefully applied to Shakespeare.

Such an idiosyncratic but dynamic conceptualization of realism shapes everything that follows, and we won't be true to Brecht's intentions if we retreat into self-conscious aesthetics or abstraction. In other words, staging 'the great realist' in the Brechtian circle of attention demands that we attend to this 'raw material'.

Provocations, Exercises and Practical Suggestions

- Ask your group to explore some of the contradictions of modern life. Three examples might be: the climate emergency versus the desire to enjoy holidays, cars and refrigerators; freedom of speech versus giving verbal offence; the need to redistribute wealth and opportunity versus the value of individual achievement and reward.
- Discuss how both sides have a point, but also how both are stuck in their own entrenched positions.
- Devise a series of short dramatic scenes in which these conflicting forces are articulated: do your best to ensure that both positions are rooted in real people. Consider two outcomes – comic and tragic – and try to understand how they might come about.
- Using the same material explore the relationship between theatrical form and political content. Attempt two different versions of the same event: one which is entirely naturalistic (set in the kitchen of a suburban house, perhaps); the second which allows for a range of locations (the North Pole, a rain forest, an Amazon warehouse, a Cabinet meeting and so on) and different dramatic forms (songs, jokes, poems, rap and so on). To what extent does new form create a space for new content?

The Great Individuals

Central to Brecht's view of Shakespeare is the questioning of the very idea of character, above all the mighty individual who strides the stage 'like a colossus' (*Julius Caesar*, 1.2.135). Brecht insisted that character isn't a fixed substance, but is shaped by circumstances and is therefore capable of change.

Brecht saw Shakespeare's central figures in historical terms, declaring that they 'anticipated the 300 years in which the individual developed himself into a capitalist' (Barnett, 2013, 119). The idea of

Elizabethan England as a stage on which the 'self-awareness of the new individual personality ... was then uncontrollably bursting out' is widely accepted, not just by conservatives championing the 'great man theory of history' but by radicals interested in historicizing such 'self-fashioning' (*BoT*, 1964, 182).

Brecht's Philosopher points out, however, that this energy isn't always positive, and that the actions of the leading figures often threaten the social order on which they depend:

> There's Lear, caught up in his own patriarchal ideas; Richard III, the dislikeable man who becomes a terrible one; Macbeth, the ambitious man tricked by witches; Antony, the libertine who gambles with world domination; Othello, whose jealousy ultimately kills him – they are all living in a new world that smashes them to pieces.
>
> (*BoP*, 2014, 57)

The same, of course, could be said of Coriolanus and, even, Hamlet. Thus, while the great individual helps drive change, the process can be damaging to both him and his world, and it was in such epoch-making contradictions that the tragic can be found. Indeed, as the Philosopher asks, 'How could there be anything more multifaceted, fascinating and important than the decline of the great ruling classes?' (*BoP*, 2014, 57).

Brecht was eager to emphasize the 'relative qualities' of these figures, the extent to which they shouldn't be seen as mighty monoliths, but something more nuanced, more complex:

> THE ACTOR If I depict a man as relatively ambitious, people are hardly likely to be grabbed by it in the same way as if I showed him to be completely consumed by ambition.
>
> THE PHILOSOPHER But in real life it's more common for people to be relatively ambitious than completely consumed by ambition, isn't it?
>
> THE ACTOR Maybe. But what about the impact we want to make?
>
> THE PHILOSOPHER You have to achieve it using something that's more likely to happen in real life. That's up to you to sort out.
>
> THE ACTOR A fine Macbeth that would make; ambitious one minute, unambitious the next, and only relatively more ambitious than Duncan. And your Hamlet: very hesitant, but

> also prone to impetuous actions, eh? And Clytemnestra: quite vindictive. Romeo: fairly in love!
>
> THE DRAMATURG Yes, more or less. You needn't laugh. In Shakespeare, Romeo's in love even before he's seen Juliet. After that he's more in love.
>
> THE ACTOR Ha! A bursting scrotum! As if other people apart from Romeo didn't have that problem, and they're no Romeos.
>
> THE PHILOSOPHER All the same, Romeo does have one. It's a great feat of realism on Shakespeare's part to have noticed that.
>
> (*BoP*, 2014, 104)

Thus, as so often, Brecht shows that if we read the texts carefully and with one eye on the real world, we will discover that Shakespeare is more realistic than we imagined, more three-dimensional. It is the perfect antidote to both romantic idealism and liberal self-indulgence.

The underlying point is that generalizations about an individual's qualities will prevent audiences understanding what has produced these qualities and where they lead. Indeed, the key to generality is, as Hegel would have put it, 'making the truth concrete':

> The more tangibly a case is presented to spectators, the easier it is for them to abstract from it ('Lear does things like that – do I do things like that?'). One particular father can be the most universal of fathers. Particularity is a mark of universality. Particularity is to be found everywhere.
>
> (*BoP*, 2014, 68)

Modern acting has largely adopted this emphasis, if largely on a personal or family level: 'Lear is this kind of father, with this kind of relationship with his daughters.' But it's the social or political arena that gets forgotten: 'Lear is this kind of king, with this kind of relationship with his subjects.'

By emphasizing such relativity, by exploring the social construction of character and its contradictions, Shakespeare's so-called 'mighty individuals' can be placed within their time and place. Thus, in his analysis of *Othello*, Brecht observes that the 'noble Moor's' 'relationship to his beloved wife reveals itself to be a relationship to a chattel' (Barnett, 2013, 119). Similarly, Lear treats his daughters as subjects whose loyalties he can command, and his demand for a hundred knights is hardly appropriate: 'What need one?' Regan asks, and with good reason too (2.2.452).

In summary, then, Brecht rejected the notion of the sovereign individual standing above the fray and wanted to 'shift the emphasis from the personal to the social' (Barnett, 2013, 120). This doesn't pre-empt our interest in the individual ('Even the wholly anti-social can be a source of enjoyment to society so long as it is presented forcefully and on the grand scale': *BoT*, 1964, 187), but he must be shown in interaction with the rest of humanity, however destructively, and such political realism is fundamental to the broader, revolutionary project of demystifying power itself.

Provocations, Exercises and Practical Suggestions

- Ask your group to devise a short scene about a powerful man who boasts of being in control of all that he surveys.
- Introduce three figures (his oncologist, his accountant and his disabled child?) that help us see him as a man like any other.
- Do what you can to show that the same man is only *relatively* powerful (his neighbour is much more powerful, he gets out of breath easily, he forgets things etc.) and only *relatively* in control (his juniors are unhappy, his company is in trouble, his deputy is plotting against him etc.). How differently does the man appear now? How much more realistic?
- Ask your group to discuss the contradictions in their own personalities (moderate in their appetites except when offered chocolate, very polite except when talking to people in call centres, dedicated to scientific rationalism except when in love etc.). Ask them to present these contradictions in a short, improvised scene.
- Take a character from Shakespeare and identify their contradictions: impetuous but hesitant; courageous and scared; moralistic but immoral etc. Ask your group to present these contradictions, again in an improvised scene.

- Discuss what these contradictions suggest about the world. Thus, Angelo in *Measure for Measure* is both puritanical, religious and cold, *and* passionate, suggestible and a dangerous risktaker: What does this say about a system of values that tries to deny what should be the simplest and most fruitful of appetites?
- Brecht insisted that 'character' is created by external forces. Ask someone from your group to describe his own character through an expression of wishes ('I want to marry my girlfriend', 'I want to play Hamlet', 'I want to be rich' and so on) and range behind him other figures in his life, such as his parents and his siblings, his teachers and voices on social media etc., and ask them to whisper in his ear their concerns and advice: 'Do this', 'Don't do that', 'Oh no, be careful', 'Yes, please do it, it'll be fun', 'I don't think you're good enough' and so on. Help the actor understand that character isn't autonomous, but is subjected to a range of external influences and social constructions.
- Do the same exercise with a character in Shakespeare.

The Working People

'Who built the Great Wall of China?' asks the 'worker who reads' in Brecht's poem of the same name (*P*, 1976, 252–3). Brecht knew that any attempt to make a fairer world had to start with the experiences of those at the bottom and it was only when drama included that perspective that it could hope to bring about social change.

It is with that in mind that we should read those figures whom Lear famously addressed as the 'poor naked wretches' (*King Lear*, 3.4.28). For when we do, we discover that Shakespeare's 'wide and universal theatre' (*As You Like It*, 2.7.138) features a vast panorama of messengers and slaves, tradesmen and craftsmen, shepherds, innkeepers, soldiers, prostitutes and others. They are often ignored in criticism and patronized on stage, but Brecht knew that they are there and that they matter. Indeed, Margot Heinemann described the way that these figures are presented in the theatre as the 'acid test' for a production that 'has assimilated the most important elements of Brecht's thinking' (1994, 249).

The Brechtian director would explore to what extent these characters' sense of humour is a defiant response to deprivation and injustice – an expression of solidarity, indeed – and the opposite of so-called 'comic relief'. They would also examine how much they are granted agency and do more than merely facilitate the actions of their 'betters'. Actors playing these characters would listen to the way that they respond to the changes happening around them and decide whether they are anticipating a better future or recalling a happier past. And both actors and directors would explore how Shakespeare presents both positions realistically and would do everything in their power to let such perspectives be articulated and shared.

In this spirit, the Brechtian director of Shakespeare's history cycles would set out to ensure that the common soldiers are presented with care, from the most hard-bitten captain to the rawest of recruits, and would share Shakespeare's insight that wars are fought for the benefit of the powerful, but it is ordinary men who pay the price. The director would also listen to the critical voices of other working people and explore how Shakespeare portrays popular rebellion, testing (for instance) Margot Heinemann's conviction that the rebel 'Jack Cade [in *Henry VI Part Two*] can be a credible peasant leader, not just a comic drunk' (1994, 250).

Working on the comedies, the director would show that the many servants, slaves, shepherds and maids have genuine agency and offer wry, sometimes satirical commentary on the actions of their betters. Turning to the tragedies and problem plays, the director would observe the way these figures so often challenge their masters, and when staging *Coriolanus* and *Julius Caesar*, whose plebeians express striking discontent with the status quo, would explore whether they are intended – as is sometimes claimed – as a demonstration of the folly of such actions or are, rather, a credible challenge to the privileges and powers of the patricians. Finally, in the late romances, they would assess the extent to which the working people are merely generic, reflecting the more exclusive makeup of the private theatres for which they were written.

It was to this end that Brecht wrote three so-called 'practice scenes' based on classical plays (*Hamlet*, *Macbeth* and Schiller's *Mary Stuart*). These give the working people a bigger voice and offer fresh perspectives on the behaviour of the ruling classes. They don't serve much purpose today, but the principle of exploring the background, perspective and attitudes of Shakespeare's commoners is an essential corrective and should be fundamental to the rehearsal process.

Rescuing these figures from what E. P. Thompson memorably dubbed 'the enormous condescension of posterity' is a theatrical revolution waiting to happen (Thompson, 1963, 13).

Provocations, Exercises and Practical Suggestions

- Improvise a series of monologues by Hamlet's valet, Cleopatra's dressmaker, Calpurnia's maid or any other invented working person. Ensure that we learn about their lives when they're not at work but also what they think about their master or mistress. See how much depth you can give them.
- Read the Carriers in 2.1 of *King Henry IV, Part One*, the Musicians in 4.5 of *Romeo and Juliet*, or the two men ordered to murder the Duke of Clarence in 1.3 of *Richard III*. Explore how much these scenes reveal about their everyday lives. Emphasize how sharp these characters are, how intelligent and how they deal with their inevitable hardships: whether it's having to wake up early in a flea-infested bed to take almost worthless goods thirty miles to market, losing their fees as musicians because of a last-minute change in their employers' lives, or having to commit a mortal sin so as to earn a living. Rehearse these scenes carefully to discover their 'raw material', and find ways of articulating and celebrating their 'bottom up' perspective.

The Epic Theatre

Brecht's superb English biographer Stephen Parker tells us that Shakespeare was 'the great forerunner of the Epic Theatre' (2014, 540). But what does the term mean and why might it be useful?

Essentially, the epic theatre is a deliberate rejection of the 'Aristotelian unities', evident above all in neo-classical eighteenth-century drama. But it was also a conscious reaction against the tidy certainties of naturalism. Such closed forms, Brecht argued, prevented an engagement with the great conflicts of his time, and denied the possibility of change. How could Zola's 'little apartment of a bourgeois' house the industrial masses? What chance did the symmetries of neo-classicism have in depicting the rise of fascism? And, surely, elegant verse couldn't articulate the raucous voices of modernity? 'Petroleum resists the five-act form' (*BoT*, 1964, 30), Brecht joked, and only a genuinely twentieth-century form could present twentieth-century realities.

In turning to Shakespeare's theatre, Brecht discovered a useful model. Its refreshingly impure theatrical style – 'Its great characters are sophisticated versions of its crude ones, its elevated language is its vulgar language refined' (*BoP*, 2014, 55) – ranged across time and place, genre and style, and gathered together a vast range of contrasting registers to create a strikingly heterogeneous form: 'One recognizes in the disjointedness of [Shakespeare's] acts', he declared, 'the disjointedness of a human life'. He found the history plays – where the epic is 'most in evidence' – 'the closest of all to life' (Heinemann, 1994, 249) and conceded that 'stylistically speaking there is nothing all that new about [his] epic theatre' (*BoT*, 1964, 75): in other words, Shakespeare had got there first.

The epic theatre isn't just broadly inclusive, it avoids simplistic notions of causality: one thing doesn't happen *because* another thing happened; more likely, both things are taking place simultaneously, and it is in this juxtaposition that meaning can be found. Thus, Brecht's Shakespeare resists both the absolute focus on the mighty individuals of romantic drama and the claustrophobic logic of the well-made play. Instead, he offers the audience the best possible chance of grasping the unpredictable nature of historical process, and suggests how alternative outcomes might have been possible.

Thus, Shakespeare's epic theatre, as articulated by Brecht, is nothing less than dialectics in practice, a continuous provoker of discussion and debate, relying as much on counterpoint as connection, a montage of intercut narrative sequences replacing the tidy unfolding of a unitary action. Consequently, everything is seen in relationship with something else, and the audience is led to exclaim:

I'd never have thought it – That's not the way – That's extraordinary, hardly believable – It's got to stop – The sufferings of this man appal me, because they are unnecessary – That's great art: nothing obvious in it – I laugh when they weep, I weep when they laugh.

(*BoT,* 1964, 71)

Indeed, in a talk introducing his radio adaptation of *Macbeth*, Brecht declared that 'Shakespeare doesn't have to think. Nor does he have to construct. With Shakespeare the spectator does the constructing':

> [He] never needs the course of a human destiny in the second act to make a fifth act possible. With him everything takes its natural course. In the lack of connection between his acts we see the lack of connection in a human destiny, when it is recounted by someone with no interest in tidying it up so as to provide an idea (which can only be a prejudice) with an argument not taken from life. There's nothing more stupid than to perform Shakespeare so that he's clear. He's by his very nature unclear. He's pure material.
> (Heinemann, 1992, 230)

It is this jagged, open-ended approach which allows the 'great realist' to shovel onto the stage all that 'raw material', those 'unvarnished representations of things he has seen' (*BoP*, 2014, 92). And so, Shakespeare's epic theatre gave Brecht a supremely valuable model for his own work, and through his eyes we can appreciate more clearly Shakespeare's own astonishing achievements.

Provocations, Exercises and Practical Suggestions

- Give each member of your group a number and ask them to go off by themselves and devise a brief episode (just two or three sentences) in the longer story of an ambitious man, who gets everything he sets out to achieve, but discovers at the end that he is still unhappy. Ask them to take it in turns to act out the episodes in sequence, and embrace the inevitable inconsistencies in style and tone. Observe the way

each one shifts perspectives, introduces secondary characters and encourages us to look afresh.
- Take your favourite play by Shakespeare and write down on separate sheets of paper the location and chief action of each scene. Explore what is left untold, what different perspectives are introduced and how the story is told in fits and starts. Consider what happens if the order of the scenes is changed and see how piecemeal the whole thing is. Imagine what a smoother form would add, but also sacrifice.

Mixed Forms

Central to Shakespeare's epic theatre is the bringing together of a wide range of forms and genres. Indeed, it was this very impurity (which shocked neo-classical critics) that appealed to Brecht the most.

The Dramaturg in the *Messingkauf* gives a vivid account of how this came about:

> The weaving together of two storylines, which Shakespeare did so brilliantly in *The Merchant of Venice*, was a technical novelty at the time – a time which was full of that kind of rapid, headlong and reckless progress. Plays were beginning to be treated as commodities, but property relations were still chaotic. Neither thoughts nor images, incidents, ideas or inventions were protected by law, the theatre was just as much of a treasure trove as life was. Its great characters are sophisticated versions of its crude ones, its elevated language is its vulgar language refined.
> (*BoP*, 2014, 55)

The historical accuracy of this could profitably be disputed, but the underlying insights – the mingling of forms and registers, the challenge to artistic and intellectual hierarchies, and treating the theatre as a place where different classes and groups can meet each other – are essential.

And so, while the conventional director of Shakespeare strives for unity, the Brechtian director looks out for the play's complicated textures and contradictory registers, and delights in seeing them play off against each other. A good example is *Measure for*

Measure, where – as we'll see – vivid social realism rubs up against biblical cadence, political calculation is countered by theological imprecation, and the sex industry shares the stage with Catholic nuns and Jacobean puritans, with all these different registers playing off against each other in the most productive way imaginable.

We shouldn't imagine that these contrasting registers follow predictable class lines: thus, Prince Hamlet and the aristocratic young Rosalind speak breathtaking prose while the shepherds Silvius and Phoebe mainly use verse. Furthermore, the neo-classicism of the Roman plays is balanced by a palpable sense of the London street, while the idealistic young lovers, Romeo and Juliet, are surrounded by the all too earthy lives of Renaissance Verona.

Robert Weimann's Brecht-inspired *Shakespeare and the Popular Tradition of the Theatre* (1978) is relevant. It argues that this impure theatrical form does more than reserve classical forms for the powerful and popular ones for the 'plebs'. Instead, Weimann insists, the two cross-fertilize each other. He also emphasizes the survival of medieval conventions, in which a direct relationship with the audience, an emphasis on word games and riddles, and a sense of communal questioning, challenging and celebration are central. He describes an area at the front of the stage for a unique, intimate even, connection with the audience, and demonstrates the lack of a clear distinction between monologue and dialogue, with direct address taking place in the middle of a scene. In this way, Weimann argued, Shakespeare featured characters from all walks of life, and gave those of lower social status a platform on which to make their voices heard.

Such diversity and inclusivity shouldn't be confused with postmodernism which, with its practice of self-consciously citing contradictory forms, has its roots in Brechtian aesthetics, but is too narrow, too *merely* aesthetic, to be of much use here: instead, the dissolution of tidy forms suggests that tidy outcomes (whether tragic or comic) can be avoided. The theatre of real life, for Brecht as for Shakespeare, is more fluid, more evasive, more struggling to be free.

Finally, of course, this multiplicity of forms is echoed in the world outside:

> The oppressors do not always appear in the same mask. The mask cannot always be stripped off in the same way. There are so many tricks for dodging the mirror that is held out. Their

military roads are termed minor roads. Their tanks are painted to look like Macduff's bushes. Their agents can show horny hands as if they were workers. Yes: it takes ingenuity to change the hunter into the quarry. What was popular yesterday is no longer so today, for the people of yesterday were not the people as it is today.

(*BoT*, 1964, 110)

Real life is endlessly complicated, endlessly changing, endlessly assuming new shapes and appearances. The theatre should do the same.

Provocations, Exercises and Practical Suggestions

- Distribute a complete set of individual scenes from a Shakespeare play and ask each member of your group to develop a brief narration of their scene, using any means to tell the story. Perform these in sequence and see how different voices, different kinds of dramatic storytelling bring out different ways of thinking.
- Ask each member to create a one-minute film (using phone cameras and simple editing, with music, visual effects etc.) of their narration: these could be linked together in a sequence to create (for example) 'the action of *Much Ado About Nothing* in seventeen short films'. The diversity of forms is the point: see what the contrasting forms reveals, but also what they obscure.

The *Fabel*

It was in the light of Brecht's commitment to social justice that he expected the director to think about why a Shakespeare play should be revived and how it might contribute to the broader struggle.

It is, of course, entirely Brechtian to recognize that material circumstances – financial resources, actors' availability, popular demand etc. – play their part in the choice of repertoire, but Brecht insisted on something else too: a sense of why we are attempting it in the first place. As Margot Heinemann explained:

> It's not enough if the director transmits something like the original production or throws light on the age when the play was written; it has to say something meaningful to modern spectators, not just to be part of a respectable cultural heritage.
>
> (Heinemann, 1994, 234)

The articulation of this is a fundamental first step.

In attempting this, however, the director needs to avoid banal analogies. Notwithstanding many claims to the contrary, Shakespeare isn't 'our contemporary' and, as we've seen, straddling past and present is a complicated business. Instead, the director should search for what Peter Brook called the 'formless hunch' (*The Guardian*, 16 March 2011), an instinct for why the action of the play might still resonate today.

Theatre publicists sometimes speak of the director's 'take', what in advertising is called 'the elevator pitch': a pithy summary of the action, and a sense of how it can be made meaningful today. And this is perhaps the best way of understanding the *fabel*, Brecht's preferred term to describe 'A play's plot as it is retold on stage from a specific point of view' (Barnett, 86, 2015). It is an account of the *action* of the play, over and above any description of the protagonists or the individual quirks of the drama, let alone the artistic nature of the treatment.

Thus, in staging *Macbeth*, the conservative director might tell (in my own words) the *fabel* of 'how a great man is trapped by three witches and his wicked wife into murdering his king and his friends, but redeemed by the greatness of his poetic imagination even as he reminds us that all human effort is meaningless'. The Brechtian, by contrast, would show that 'the path towards dictatorial murder starts with a conscience-stricken act of regicide, moves on to the fratricidal killing of Banquo, expands to the murder of Macduff's wife and children and culminates in the apocalyptic order to "hang those who talk of fear"'. Such a production would also show the gathering opposition to Macbeth's nihilism and make plain that he is defeated by the forces of the future. In brief, in settling on the *fabel,* Brechtian directors decide on what story they want the audience to see.

Let five productions suggest the ways that a *fabel* has been articulated, but sometimes misunderstood. Thus, less than a decade after the defeat of Hitler, the Berliner Ensemble's posthumous production of Brecht's adaptation of *Coriolanus* told of a populist warmongering leader who became an 'enemy of the people', proving that no-one, however mighty, is 'indispensable'. Then, John Barton and Peter Hall's staging of *The Wars of the Roses* for the RSC in 1963 showed how aristocratic dissent created historic fissures in English society, and told a story of English division and struggle, but also suggested a new and better way of doing things. And, finally, Peter Brook's *A Midsummer Night's Dream* in 1970 evoked the hallucinogenic visions of the time by exploring the subconscious in the behaviour of its protagonists: love and sex, in Brook's *fabel*, are horribly confusing, and dreams of bliss and nightmares are interchangeable.

More recently, the value of the *fabel* (let us call it 'the take') has changed, and direct parallels and formal innovations have largely replaced the analysis of dramatic action that Brecht wanted. Thus, the New York Public Theater's 2017 revival of *Julius Caesar* presented a version of the recently elected Donald Trump in the title role and examined the responses to the emergence of anti-democratic tendencies in the leadership of the Republic; Phyllida Lloyd's all female, prison-set trilogy of *Julius Caesar, Henry IV* and *The Tempe*st in 2016 made a powerful statement about the patriarchy as the fight for female autonomy became more urgent; and, finally, Rob Hastie's production of *Much Ado About Nothing* in 2022 demonstrated a robust and infectious commitment to the inclusion of disabled people in the classical theatre.

These different revivals resonated with their audience in different ways, but all made the plays feel peculiarly alive. If the political content of the last two was more a consequence of innovative casting than an interrogation of the story itself, they nevertheless championed an alternative perspective on these monuments of 'high culture'. There are dangers involved – above all making the play a mere social media campaign – and the modern theatre must be careful to avoid introspection. But establishing the *fabel* is essential.

Provocations, Exercises and Practical Suggestions

- Ask your group to devise a *fabel* for a Shakespeare play. This should be no longer than 50 words, with no names, adjectives or adverbs, just job titles, social relationships and plenty of transitive verbs: 'This is the story of an A who does B to C, D and E and is eventually defeated by F, G and H.'
- Ask your group to take it in turns to present their *fabel*. If sufficiently anonymized ('a king' rather than 'King Richard III'), ask the others to guess which play is being presented.
- Explore what happens when the key terms are changed: thus, what's the difference between 'Macbeth murders King Duncan, but is defeated by forces led by Duncan's son' and 'Macbeth murders everyone who gets in his way, and is eventually defeated by a gathering opposition of exiles'? Different *fabels* result in different productions.

Changing the Text

One of the knotty questions that all directors of Shakespeare face is settling on the text that is to be used. How much should the politically minded director cut, change or restructure these revered old works?

Brecht's youthful enthusiasm was palpable: 'I've read Shakespeare's *Antony & Cleopatra*, a splendid drama which really gripped me', he wrote in his early diaries (D, 1979, 15). Elsewhere, he praised the 'monumentality of Shakespeare' (D, 1979, 112) and there are other expressions of almost childlike awe. He didn't regard the plays as 'perfect', however, and increasingly relished their many inconsistencies. Above all, he was eager to suggest that the playwright's approach was improvisational:

> THE ACTOR From your description it sounds like Shakespeare was adding a new scene pretty much every day.

THE DRAMATURG Exactly. I think they were experimenting. They were experimenting, just like Galileo in Florence at that time and Bacon in London, and that is why it's right to produce the plays experimentally.
THE ACTOR That will be seen as sacrilege.
THE DRAMATURG The plays owe their existence to sacrilege.
THE ACTOR But as soon as you alter them in any way, you lay yourself open to the charge of treating them as less than perfect.
THE DRAMATURG That's just a mistaken idea of perfection, nothing more.

(*BoP*, 2014, 900)

If this is true, and if these plays are, as he says elsewhere, the product of 'barbaric' times, aren't we in our rights to experiment further and rework them for our own ends?

It was in a perhaps too gnomic attempt to answer this question that Brecht touched on the subject in his insightful dialogue about the first scene of *Coriolanus*:

W. Can we amend Shakespeare?
B. I think we can amend Shakespeare, if we can amend him.

(*BoT*, 1964, 259)

This can easily be misunderstood. Brecht isn't saying that we should only 'amend' Shakespeare if we're clever enough to improve it; rather, that we should only attempt such changes if it helps the play speak in new and different ways, especially by increasing its dialectical content and opening the action up to fruitful contradictions. And this isn't a question of just adding a few lines, it's about changing what the plays do and how they do it. A perfect example might be Brecht's suggestion of an additional, dialectical episode in *Julius Caesar*: 'The tyrant's murder by Brutus is alienated if during one of his monologues accusing Caesar of tyrannical motives, he himself maltreats a slave waiting on him' (*BoT*, 1964, 143). This reminds us that Brutus' rebellion comes from within the ruling elite, and isn't (necessarily) popular.

Although in the modern theatre, non-spoken action (dance, slapstick, mime) is common, it's only recently that directors (occasionally) introduce new text, sometimes the odd word (for clarity or to avoid offence), sometimes more extensively. Occasionally, entire new scenes are written, especially in the less well-known or less revered scenes (the British comedian Stewart Lee recently rewrote the Porter in *Macbeth* at the RSC in 2023). But although directors are eager to offer fresh visions of the plays, they are usually reluctant to change the words themselves. Perhaps they've adopted Brecht's caution: see, for example, his comment about *Hamlet* that 'few textual changes are needed' (*L*, 1990, 481) or his eventual adoption of the unaltered text of *Coriolanus* (*J*, 1993, 460). More likely, they lack the self-confidence to 'amend' Shakespeare in the ways that Brecht suggested.

Another way of making changes is cutting the text, which directors often do to make performances short enough for modern tastes (the plays, which are substantial longer than most of his contemporaries, were almost certainly cut originally). The more incomprehensible references are also frequently dispensed with – perhaps subtly, perhaps forcefully – with mixed results. Thus, when directing *King Lear* in 2002 I trimmed Edgar's speeches as Poor Tom as a way of ensuring that his comments stood the best chance of being understood: my logic was that under the conditions of Jacobean censorship his extravagant ramblings obscured his political critique, and that with a prudent trim his concerns could become more legible. In the process I sacrificed some of Shakespeare's mystery, but I did achieve greater political clarity. Laser sharp surgery to save the patient, perhaps?

More worrying, perhaps, is the tendency to dispense with several of the 'minor' roles, which can have a fatal impact on the dialectical structure. Some cuts are more drastic still, and a recent production of *The Merchant of Venice* (2022, Sam Wanamaker Playhouse), eager to alienate the play's antisemitism, bravely dispensed with the entire last act in which the Christian romance story bears fruit, changing (in what I thought was a productive experiment) the overall thrust of the play.

Directors also increasingly cut passages which they find uncomfortable. Certainly, as the father of a disabled young man, I dislike Oberon's speech at the end of *A Midsummer Night's Dream*:

And the blots of Nature's hand
Shall not in their issue stand.
Never mole, harelip, nor scar,
Nor mark prodigious, such as are
Despisèd in nativity,
Shall upon their children be.

(5.1.395)

I understand that this is intended as a blessing (which a sophisticated production might be able to convey), but it should probably be dropped nowadays, especially since it is likely to be regarded as the view of the playwright himself.

Similarly, Claudio's assertion towards the end of *Much Ado About Nothing* that he would marry his unknown bride 'were she an Ethiope' (5.4.38) suggests barely endurable humiliation if she turned out to be Black: the fact that this wouldn't have seemed as offensive in the 1590s shouldn't prevent us from cutting it today. The crucial thing is to proceed with our eyes open, aware of the historical nature of what is written, even as we question its underlying values.

Other interventions include shifting the position of scenes and speeches, or taking episodes from different plays and transposing them into the action. As a student, I once experimented (unsuccessfully) with inserting the brothel scenes from *Pericles* into *Measure for Measure* and Brecht took material from *Julius Caesar* and placed it in his adaptation of *Coriolanus*. The essential point is that all such changes are more than merely aesthetic: they have an impact on how the play is received. In other words, we should only change Shakespeare if we think carefully about what we're doing.

Provocations, Exercises and Practical Suggestions

- Ask a member of your group to read aloud the final ten lines of a familiar Shakespeare text. Experiment with rewriting them, either to turn a happy ending into a sad one or to make a sad one happy.
- Using the same play, write a six-line epilogue (perhaps in blank verse?) which provides a moral or simply offers a different perspective on what we have seen.

- Pick a shortish scene, count how many words are in it and set out to cut 10 per cent. Describe what you have lost, but also what is gained.
- Using the same scene, write 10 per cent of fresh dialogue to ensure that a wider range of perspectives is evident.
- Choose another scene and highlight the words or phrases that members of your group consistently don't understand (without using a glossary). Explore cutting an occasional word, modernizing one or two others, and see whether that makes the text seem alive again. In other words, wrestle with the text to make it understandable.

2

Rehearsing

The experienced director knows that however incisive their ideas might be, however much they have thought about the play and where it comes from, however carefully they have articulated their *fabel* and prepared a script for the production, putting it all into practice is a very different matter. It's time to enter the rehearsal room and see how Brecht can help us 'on the floor'.

The Brechtian Director

The records that exist of Brecht's rehearsals are revealing.

In the early years, like many a young director, he was impulsive, confrontational and impatient, with little understanding of what professional actors need and no real engagement with his audience beyond the wish to shock. As his skill developed, however, so did his self-confidence, and his work in the early 1930s was increasingly successful. In exile, he was unable to direct at a professional level but, once back in Berlin and rehearsing the magnificent productions on which his reputation is built, he showed striking levels of care and collaboration. There seems to have been nothing abstract about his methods and he progressed by an empirical process of trial and error: after all, as he liked to say, 'The proof of the pudding is in the eating'.

Brecht's rehearsals were exploratory in spirit, if infused with temperament and laughter, provocation and debate. Received opinions were challenged, just as new ideas were subjected to careful evaluation. Brecht examined everything that was played out in front of him with a penetrating gaze, and encouraged others to do the same, subjecting each moment of the action to three key questions:

1. Does it help to tell the story?
2. Does it show the way the world works?
3. Does it explain how the world has changed and can be changed again?

Such questioning was particularly useful when rehearsing classical drama, where Brecht hoped his audience would experience the play as the product of its time, but also as something which could speak to their own lives.

He went out of his way to listen to the opinions not just of his associates and assistants but of actors and designers, even secretaries, drivers, technicians and cleaners. He wanted to create a theatre that was accessible to audiences from all backgrounds, especially those traditionally excluded, and was determined to listen to the 'experts of everyday life'. The Berliner Ensemble was hardly a cooperative and Brecht was the ultimate arbiter, but he knew that if its productions were to be robust and hold their own, they had to stand up to robust scrutiny.

In this spirit, the Brechtian director makes rehearsals as exploratory as possible. Although the director will have read the play carefully and thought through the issues that it raises, they won't come to the first day of rehearsals with a fully thought through account of every detail. Instead, they'll work empirically, inductively indeed, making decisions informed by what they see unfold in front of them. They'll start from a blank sheet and 'insist that at any one time several solutions be considered' (Barnett, 2015a, 10). This isn't always easy and requires patience and courage, but produces the liveliest results.

Like all the best directors, Brecht displayed a striking combination of patience and impatience, silent observation and voluble intervention, precise instruction and jokey provocation. He watched the action with detachment, even when rehearsing his own writing, continually questioning what the writer had written, recalling perhaps the wooden donkey in his study with the sign saying, 'Even I must understand it.' We need to do the same when rehearsing Shakespeare.

Brecht regarded actors as 'active co-producers of meaning', and this 'perpetual call to action was designed to engage both mind and body in the exploration not only of their own roles, but of the roles of the rest of the ensemble' (Barnett, 2015a, 13). He banned abstract discussion and insisted that his actors should make their suggestions by physical proposition, not verbal debate. After all, as he liked to say, 'The truth is concrete'.

Brecht had a particular talent for illustrating his ideas physically, as one actress recalled: 'He always ran up on to the stage. But he didn't want us to copy him. He wanted to provide a spark' (Barnett, 2015a, 34). What's more, he didn't 'tell the actor what to do or how to speak the lines but gave him a social reference point that could stimulate a set of responses' (Barnett, 2015a, 32). It's a skill that I have tried to develop in my own work.

Although I usually have a script to hand, I tend not to look at it when rehearsing. Indeed, I encourage everyone to watch what is happening in front of them as if it was being played for the first time, in all its incompleteness. It's generally a mistake to rehearse with the *idea* of the play in your head; what's more productive is to engage with a particular group of actors at a particular moment in time and see what they bring. Such attention is essential if we are to create something fresh and alive.

Brecht devised several exercises for actors, especially useful for performers not accustomed to his approach. These should be approached with two caveats. First, they are only useful if they help reveal fresh perspectives on playing the text: no one buys a theatre ticket to watch an acting exercise. Second, they must be allied to a broader understanding of what lies beyond the rehearsal room: indeed the main point of these exercises is to help actors perform with one eye on the real world. I will detail some of them as we proceed.

Provocations, Exercises and Practical Suggestions

- Rehearse a short scene from a play by Shakespeare that no one in your group knows well, and ask those not participating to watch the action without a script. Encourage them to raise a hand every time they don't

understand what is happening, and consider what needs to be adjusted to make the action clear.
- Rehearse another scene, perhaps in a play your group knows well, and emphasize its social aspect. Thus, working on the encounter between the Prince and the Gravedigger in *Hamlet* (5.1.61–205) look at how two men from opposite poles of the social sphere interact with each other. Ask who knows more about the other's life and what lessons they offer each other. Instead of regarding them as introverted individuals, treat them as people experiencing the world in interaction with others (even, ultimately, Yorick's skull). And explore Horatio's role in all this too.
- Examine the changes that happen during the scene, and consider how the characters end the scene different than when they started. Define the cause and nature of this change.
- Ask the actors to comment on each line of a (different) scene in *Hamlet*, with the prefix: 'In the same way that …' with a reference to an everyday event in the modern world. Thus, 'In the same way that a man is unsure whether to buy a blue or a green shirt, so Hamlet is unclear whether he wants to continue living.' A more serious version might be 'In the same way that a man is unsure about whether he wants to stay in his marriage, so Hamlet is unclear whether he wants to continue living.' These parallels are inexact, but that's the point: explore what's different, unique perhaps, about Hamlet's inquiry, and your group will start to sense the particular and historical nature of Shakespeare's play.

Actors and Casting

It is sometimes said that casting is 90 per cent of the director's job. Brecht certainly took great care in assembling his company and his work is impossible without performers of real quality. Beyond the obvious – if hard to define – criteria of acting ability, casting in the Brechtian theatre depends on two key qualities.

The first is finding actors interested in representing people in the round, prepared to show the part's unattractive features alongside its appealing ones, and capable of performing with objectivity and understanding. The Brechtian actor will demonstrate how an 'evil' character is capable of kindness, but also how a 'good' character isn't always 'good'. If he's playing Hamlet, he'll make it clear that he is both a philosopher and a prince, an active young man and paralysed by self-doubt, and that for all his seeming humanity he is capable of surprising brutality. Likewise, the actress playing Rosalind will acknowledge her class-based contempt for the love-sick Phoebe even while showing that she is forging a more egalitarian form of love. And, finally, an actor attempting Julius Caesar will reveal the character's superstitious and dictatorial instincts even as he allows for human sympathy as the victim of the assassins' blades.

The second is to resist frankly racist, sexist, ableist or otherwise stereotypical ideas: thus, Juliet doesn't have to be a blonde, an effeminate Macbeth is possible and Hamlet can be 'fat and scant of breath' (5.2.269). All ethnicities are welcome, and the defying of preconceptions is essential. But, the Brechtian director will also attend to social detail: thus, the episode in *Henry V* when the disguised king meets the common soldiers (4.1) is at its most powerful if the physiognomy, accent and bearing of the actors involved makes the class difference clear; and when casting Jack Cade in *Henry VI Part Two* the director would do well to find an actor who can embody Cade's populist appeal, and a typical Etonian is hardly ideal. In other words, class isn't an optional extra.

Paradoxically, Brecht was also attracted to casting against type. As David Barnett explains, 'to Brecht, the mark of real actors was that they desired and were able to portray people very different from themselves' (2015a, 12). Thus, in the 'Short Organum' Brecht argues that 'if the part is played by someone of the opposite sex the sex of the character will be more clearly brought out; if it is played by a comedian, whether comically or tragically, it will gain fresh aspects' (*BoT*, 1964, 197). And when thinking about *Coriolanus*, Brecht wanted the defiantly proletarian Ernst Busch in the title role (Hayman, 1983, 356). Such a distance between the actor and the role can allow for a vivid demonstration of attitude and behaviour: 'This is how this person might have behaved in such circumstances', the actor suggests.

The essential point is that casting shapes meaning. Thus, physically disabled performers are increasingly employed to represent characters with no indication of disability (and vice versa); 'colour-blind casting' has dramatically broadened the ethnic range of the performers, often with no specific determinant in the character; women play men (not just the iconic roles, as has long happened, but others too) and productions increasingly explore other non-binary identities; finally (though not always successfully), modern directors have occasionally shared Brecht's observation that 'the great comedians have always been the best character actors' (*BoT*, 1964, 68).

There are good reasons for these decisions, but they sometimes shed more light on the theatre than on the world of the fiction itself. As early as 1920, Brecht went to the heart of this paradox, in declaring that he'd like to mount a production of *Hamlet* played by clowns:

> The idea would be to bring reality back to the things on the stage. For God's sake, it's the *things* that need to be criticised – the action, word, gestures – not their execution.
>
> (*D*, 1979, 33)

And so, innovative casting should do more than just give a particular demographic a chance. It should help audiences engage with the realities of the world: 'the *things* ... not their execution'.

We need to be cautious, however, before we embrace this too fervently. The idea that any actor can play any part usually results in blandness, a draining away of the distinctive features of class, age and life experience. And although Helene Weigel was the daughter of a successful Jewish accountant (murdered in the Holocaust), she was superbly cast as Mother Courage, the (mostly) impoverished small-time tradeswoman trying to survive the Thirty Years War: she had the intelligence and understanding to present the part in all its contradictions, but was credible throughout in terms of age, build and physiognomy. These things still matter.

It is sometimes assumed that the Berliner Ensemble was a collective of artists brought together by shared dreams and visions, but lacking in quality or charisma. As early as 1930, however, Brecht urged caution:

> Some theatres have tried to foster an 'ensemble spirit'. What this usually boils down to is that all the actors are expected to sacrifice their own egoism for 'the good of the play'. It is actually much better to mobilize this egoism in each and every actor.
>
> (*BoT*, 2015, 58)

If anything, the Ensemble was a constellation of stars and Brecht, like Shakespeare, wrote plays which cannot be properly realized without them. Indeed, David Barnett quotes one of Brecht's assistants explaining that 'ensemble doesn't mean everyone has the same ability, only that every role has the correct actor and that they are all in balance with each other' (2015b, 11). It's certainly striking to read of the Ensemble's single-minded focus:

> Of course the stage of a realistic theatre must be peopled by live, three-dimensional, self-contradictory people, with all their passions, unconsidered utterances and actions. The stage is not a hothouse or a zoological museum full of stuffed animals.
>
> (*BoT*, 1964, 235)

Acting is acting, whatever the purpose to which it is put.

The mature Brecht spoke of actors with considerable affection. As Benno Besson recalled, he had 'respect for everyone on stage' (Kleber and Visser, 1991, 115). What's more, he was surprisingly undogmatic: indeed, as John Willett tells us, one leading actress 'never read Brecht's theoretical works' (*BoT*, 1964, 236n) and I was told (by someone who was there) that Helene Weigel dismissed the alienation effect to a group of English actors as 'a silly idea that Bert came up with to stop people from overacting'. It was the brave, bold, powerfully theatrical performances of the leads, and the superbly individualized and expressive acting of the others, that most impressed. And it's that which we should emulate as we attempt our own Brechtian approach to Shakespeare.

Provocations, Exercises and Practical Suggestions

- Imagine you are casting Hamlet. What happens to the story if you cast Barack Obama in the title role? How different is it if you cast the young Donald Trump? Or Kamala Harris, indeed? In other words, casting affects meaning.
- Similarly, cast the two named leads in *Romeo and Juliet* in a way that feels appropriate in traditional terms. Now, cast them as 'badly' as possible (or simply swap genders). What do these two approaches offer? What is lost? What is gained?

- Consider how you would cast the pimp Pompey in *Measure for Measure*. Search the text for any hints you can find about his class, his education, his way of life, but also about his energy, his defiance and his optimism. Who is good casting for this? Who is bad What do you gain by each, and what do you lose?
- If you like, do the same exercises using members of the group.

The Story

'Everything hangs on the "story"', Brecht declared (using the English word): 'It is the heart of the theatrical performance' (*BoT*, 1964, 200). Indeed, the preparatory notes to many of his plays chart the action in meticulous detail and his productions focused, above all, on the narrative arc. Telling the story clearly provides the production with its guiding light.

Brecht's emphasis was hardly new. Aristotle had argued in *The Poetics* that an 'imitation of an action' lay at the heart of tragedy and Brecht agreed that 'narrative is the soul of drama' (*BoT*, 1964, 183). And when asked by a women's magazine which book had influenced him the most, he replied drily, 'The Bible. Don't laugh': no doubt partly because of its dedication to storytelling. Indeed, his insistence on the sequencing of units of action, often disconnected and presented in counterpoint to each other, but always purposeful in their own terms, was genuinely radical at the time, even in its adoption of an ancient dramatic principle.

The story's chief value was that it showed the possibility of change: 'You can't step twice into the same river', the philosopher Heraclitus argued, and wisdom shows that nothing lasts forever, especially the fixed hierarchies of the world. By dramatizing the collision of opposites and carefully charting the outcome, a dramatic story suggests the way the world changes, and how it can be changed again. 'For it is what happens *between* people', Brecht insisted, 'that provides them with all the material that they can discuss, criticize, alter' (*BoT*, 1964, 200). And it's only when this is visible that we can make any claim as to what the play is 'about': define, indeed, our *fabel*.

Thus, instead of saying (in my own words) that *Richard II* is 'about a weak king with a poetic soul', we should say that in the play a 'weak king with a poetic soul is deposed by a very different kind of leader'. Similarly, when we come to stage the (so-called) 'mechanicals' in *A Midsummer Night's Dream* we can tell 'the story of a group of poorly educated tradesmen who are selected to stage (for financial reward) a play for the wedding of their aristocratic masters, which is temporarily threatened when their leading actor goes missing; and when they do come to perform it, their masters condescend to them, even as they're being entertained by their best efforts'. It is only when these interactions are clearly told that the play's social content becomes visible.

In practical terms this means subjecting each moment of the story to careful analysis: 'Play one thing after another', Brecht insisted, and a production should be careful not to blur the individual actions that bring about change. Indeed, one of the Berliner Ensemble's leading actresses recalls that her understanding of character was defined, above all, by the concepts of 'turning point' and 'break': the crucial moments in a performance when we see dynamic change.

Brecht expected the actor to highlight the individual moments of decision. Thus, he wanted the actor to suggest that Hamlet *could* have killed Claudius when he was praying, Cordelia in the first scene of *King Lear could* have said that she loved her father even more than her sisters, Isabella in *Measure for Measure could* have decided to sleep with Angelo to save her brother's life, and so on. Thus, the choices which shape the course of the action are played in such a way that the audience cares about the outcome, and learns how change occurs. Alternatives are always possible.

To this end, Brecht encouraged his actors to tell the story in the third person. Thus, the actor rehearsing the prince might say: 'Discovering his uncle at prayer, Hamlet considers stabbing him from behind and so take his revenge, but decides instead – aware that Claudius in mid-prayer would go straight to heaven – to postpone his death until the revenge is more effective.' Or Cordelia could say: 'Instead of competing with her sisters in her declaration of love to her father, Cordelia decides not to play the game.' The effect is simple: it heightens the dramatic jeopardy, but it also helps focus on the decision itself: the engine not just of the plot, but history too.

Brecht's theatre set out to 'make the reproduction of real-life events the purpose of art and thereby make something conducive of the spectators' critical attitude toward them?' (J, 1993, 81). It is the unfolding of the story, moment by moment, beat by beat, decision by decision, that allows this to happen. Don't ignore it.

Provocations, Exercises and Practical Suggestions

- Distil a scene to its simple actions. Ensure that these describe what happens *between* the characters and dispense with all adjectives or adverbs. You could even avoid proper names and describe people by their social rank: thus, 'The Duke [in *King Lear*, 3.7] orders his servants to bring in the Earl and strap him to a chair' and so on.
- Ask two members of your group to present these bullet points in a brief performance, taking it in turns to enact each one with the simplest suggestion of what is being described.
- Rehearse a different scene and encourage the actors to represent every beat, however minor, of the unfolding story. Ask the actors to focus on those moments when the character decides on an individual course of action, or even, Hamlet-like, opts to do nothing. Above all emphasize the way that things continually change.
- Insist that the actors don't gloss over such moments of decision and find ways of sharing them with the audience. The careful charting of such choices ('He did this, not that'; 'She decided to come here, not stay there') reveals the way things have changed and can change again.
- Ask the actors a series of simple Stanislavskian questions: 'What does your character want?' 'What stops them getting what they want?' and 'What do they do to achieve it?' But supplement these with more social ones: 'How does your character earn a living?', 'What are the material conditions of his/her lives?' and 'What are the rules that govern their world?' Explore how an essentially psychological approach doesn't necessarily conflict with a more social one, but explore what Brecht offers that Stanislavski doesn't.

Gestus

If a play tells the story of a world in change and if the audience is to understand how that change comes about, it must show people *doing* things to each other.

In Brecht's theatre this takes the form of what he called *gestus*. Brecht insisted that this Latinate term refers to something more than mere gesture or emphatic movement. Instead, it's a physical embodiment of human relationships, offering the audience a visible manifestation of the underlying social structures. And an actor who expresses each *gest* clearly and decisively will perform with a certain transparency of intent.

Brecht offered a useful definition of *gestus* in the 'Short Organum':

> Physical attitude, tone of voice and facial expression are all determined by a social gest: the characters are cursing, flattering, instructing one another, and so on ... These expressions of a gest are usually highly complicated and contradictory, so that they cannot be rendered by any single word and the actor must take care that in giving his image the necessary emphasis he does not lose anything, but emphasizes the entire complex.
>
> (*BoT*, 1964, 198)

The physical articulation of the *gest* gives clarity to the social transaction, and helps us see the characters in relationship with each other.

Defining *gests* helps make a production purposeful. Instead of concentrating on their own individual performances, the actors will work together on clarifying the scene, moment by moment, beat by beat, and adjust their performances accordingly. If the result is somewhat artificial, like paintings of Bible scenes or episodes from the classics, such richly embodied interactions help the audience engage both imaginatively and within the historical context. The audience watches the play *both* as the product of its time and as a living, breathing event.

There are various scales of *gest*. An individual character can embody a *gest*: thus, instead of asking, 'Who is Macbeth?', the Brechtian actor wants to know, 'What does Macbeth do?' Instead of wondering, 'How does Rosalind feel?', the actress will enquire, 'How does Rosalind communicate her feelings at this particular moment?' And instead of questioning, 'What is it like to be a powerful but insecure king', the Brechtian director asks, 'How does Claudius use the power that he yields to shore up his own position?' In other words, by seeing characters in relationships with each other, the audience can observe the shifts in power and status, wealth and class, duty and solidarity, that, one way or another, bring about change.

An individual scene is made up of a number of *gests*. Thus the first scene of *King Lear* shows a rapid deterioration in Lear's status: it starts with the *gest* of the mighty King entering with full pomp, giving an order that he is confident will be obeyed ('Attend the lords of France and Burgundy, Gloucester', 1.1.33) and announcing his regal intentions (35–54). The first substantial shift in *gest*, the first real change, comes with 'But now our joy' (82), where the king lets his personal feelings show. And soon *gest* follows *gest*, from that of the indulgent father (94–5), the wounded lover, the grandiloquent magus (110–21), the disobeyed patriarch (125), the monarch facing down rebellion (155), right through to the bitterly angry and isolated king, who has triggered a potential conflict with his kingdom's mighty neighbour, France (263–6). Each of these changing attitudes, Brecht insisted, should be made visible.

Gests can be detected on a more intimate scale too. Indeed, according to Brecht, every interaction between people on stage can be expressed as a *gest* and, in analysing and staging the text, the director and actors should articulate the continuously changing relationships in a series of continuously changing *gests*: 'This is what it looks like being sceptical about the king's intentions', shows the actor playing Kent. 'And this is what it looks like to dare to speak up.'

These *gests* will be shaped by individual detail: thus, the actor playing Kent can suggest that it's easier for an Earl to voice concerns than a peasant; but he can also show that his ultimate role is to be a servant to the King, not simply an advisor. The precise nature of these moments will vary from actor to actor, but by embodying the particular social relationship, the actor stands the best chance of communicating what is going on.

Typically, of course, *gests* can also be observed in the real world. Thus, watching the catastrophe that was engulfing Europe in the 1930s, Brecht described how 'the pomp of the Fascists, taken at its face value, has a hollow gest, the gest of mere pomp, a featureless phenomenon':

Men strutting instead of walking, a certain stiffness, a lot of colour, self-conscious sticking out of chests, etc. All this could be the gest of some popular festivity, quite harmless, purely factual and therefore to be accepted. Only when the strutting takes place over corpses do we get the social gest of fascism.

(*BoT*, 1964, 105)

As usual with Brecht, the real world sheds light on the theatre, and vice versa.

Provocations, Exercises and Practical Suggestions

- Draw up a list of Lear's shifting relationships in the first scene of *King Lear* and act out each new *gest*. Take a simple photograph of each one and print them out. Then, shuffle them and distribute them in a fresh sequence and see if an outsider can grasp the essential of what is going on at each moment. If anything is unclear, explore what might need to change.

- Choose a scene from Shakespeare and identify as many individual *gests* as you can. Experiment with playing them in sequence, and preface each with the statement: 'This is what [the name of the character] looks like when he is [e.g.] begging for mercy / condemning someone to death / seducing someone, etc.'

Actioning

A useful technique has been developed in the British theatre as a way of encouraging *gestic* playing. In 'actioning', as it's called, every moment of the drama is defined as a specific 'action', and actors are asked to identify the transitive verb that best describes what their character is doing to another character.

We could take two examples from the scene in *Much Ado About Nothing* when Beatrice and Benedick are left in the church after Hero has been publicly disgraced (4.1.255–334). Thus, in actioning, the actress would ask, what is Benedick *doing to* Beatrice with the opening line: 'Lady Beatrice, have you wept all this while?' Is he 'challenging' her? 'seducing' her? 'comforting' her? 'quizzing' her, or what? Deciding on this will subtly shape how the line is played and what the audience sees. It's significant that in the very next line Benedick says that he doesn't want her to weep, suggesting that he is 'challenging' more than simply 'expressing sympathy'. (And, of course, such a challenge is socially constructed: Benedick is taking on the role of the gallant who will champion the innocent virgin's honour.)

Indeed, the power (and pleasure) of the scene depends on the nature of this initial action. The climax comes when Beatrice answers Benedick's request ('Come, bid me do anything for thee') with the simplest of instructions, 'Kill Claudio!' (287–8). But what is her 'action' here? Is she 'commanding' him, 'challenging' him, 'exciting' him, 'humiliating' him, 'seducing' him? All, in their different ways, are playable, but the actress will need to make up her mind, and answer the key question: what story are we trying to tell? Certainly, if we allow Benedick to open the scene with a certain swagger ('He is mansplaining to her', perhaps?), Beatrice's challenge cuts to the heart of his masculine peacocking.

But even this should be subjected to challenge when, in true Brechtian spirit, the actress playing Beatrice shows the action with sufficient (comic) awareness (what we will soon call 'alienation') that the audience glimpses the dreadful consequences if her command to 'kill Claudio' was actually carried out. Such dialectical thinking is the stuff of the Brechtian theatre and the careful playing out of the individual *gests*, the actions and social attitudes of each moment, makes it visible. As Brecht argued, 'It is the inaccurate way in which happenings between human beings are represented that restricts our pleasure' (*BoT*, 1964, 183). Actioning is a good way of preventing such inaccuracy.

Provocations, Exercises and Practical Suggestions

- Look at 4.1 of *Much Ado* and 'action' every speech. Remember to use transitive verbs throughout and no adjectives or adverbs.

- Rehearse the scene without the text (or names) but just describing the actions: 'A does B to C', 'X does Y to Z' and so on.
- Rehearse the scene speaking these actions aloud before saying every line.
- Experiment with subtly changing an action (e.g. change 'Beatrice *demands* that Benedick should kill Claudio' to 'Beatrice *suggests* that Benedick should kill Claudio') and see how the performance subtly changes.

The Alienation Effect

Of all Brecht's theatrical terms, the 'alienation effect' is probably the best known, but also the most misunderstood. The German compound word – *Verfremdungseffekt* – literally means 'the effect that makes things strange', and so 'estrangement' is perhaps better than the usual 'alienation', with its association with cruelty and exclusion. Whichever word we use, the phenomenon is evident in 'the Chinese theatre, the Spanish classical theatre, the popular theatre of Brueghel's day and the Elizabethan theatre' (*BoT*, 1964, 135); it is certainly fundamental to Shakespeare's, which Brecht described as being 'full of alienation effects!' (*BoP*, 2014, 58).

Alienation can be found in the texts themselves. Look, for example, at *Romeo and Juliet* and see how the Nurse, the Friar, the illiterate servant Peter, the musicians and the many household servants help set the jewel of aristocratic love in the mud of a very real world, the same world which makes it so hard for the young lovers to pull down the wall standing between their families. Shakespeare's inclusion of everyday experience encourages us to see their romantic idealism with a degree of objectivity: we are alienated from it. And the fact that Romeo is already in love with another girl before he spots Juliet (what Brecht meant when he joked that Romeo had a 'bursting scrotum', *BoP*, 2014, 104) allows us to see his newfound passion with sceptical, if affectionate, detachment. This is what teenage boys are like, we smile knowingly, even as we are swept up in the action.

Another example is the episode (2.5) in the third part of the *Henry VI* trilogy which juxtaposes the Son who discovers to his horror that he has killed his Father with the Father who is appalled to learn that he has killed his Son. Both killings, Shakespeare shows, were motivated by personal gain even as they resonate with the tragic cadences of primal sacrifice. But this symmetrical tableau of interlocking events, watched over by the weak king sat on a molehill, is also a powerful emblem of the catastrophe sweeping the land. Indeed, little shows more vividly the impact of civil war on ordinary people (as England was to discover in the 1640s), and this double refraction, this *alienation*, makes us examine the action of the ruling classes with fresh eyes. If this is what civil war means, who could possibly think it was a good idea?

A fresh reading can also create the alienation effect, as can be seen in Brecht's take on *Hamlet*. He had seen the play in a touring Swedish production and declared that it had (almost) 'the crudest plot' Shakespeare ever wrote. His account makes the familiar seem strange and the strange familiar, to striking effect:

> Hamlet is simply an idealist thrown out of kilter when he collides with the real world, the idealist who turns into a cynic. The question is not: to act or nor to act, but to keep silent or not to keep silent, to give approval or not to give approval.

We can protest that this is oversimplistic, but Brecht helps us understand something about the change the central character undergoes and how the bloodbath at the end is possible:

> All that thinking and planning, all the cramped contortions of his conscience finish up uncertainly, fortuitously, in a shambles of intrigue and planlessness. Still waiting for corroboration of his suspicion that they are plotting against his life, Hamlet dies, with several murders to his own credit. This woeful butchery, devoid of morality, the self-destruction of a clan, only a theatre like the Elizabethan could have produced.
>
> <div align="right">(<i>J</i>, 1993, 118)</div>

It certainly offers a different view of the familiar text: 'Faced with irrational practices [Hamlet's] reason is utterly unpractical', Brecht explained, 'He falls a tragic victim to the discrepancy between such reasoning and such action' (*BoT*, 1964, 202). This isn't the only way of reading the play, Brecht knew, but it provides the basis for critical intervention.

Actors are frequently mystified by the alienation effect, not necessarily helped by Brecht insistence that 'to produce A-effects the actor has to discard whatever means he has learnt of getting the audience to identify itself with the characters which he plays' *(BoT, 1964, 193)*. I can best explain it as an approach to acting which by constantly keeping the part at a distance allows the actor to highlight contradictory details and create a space for judgement. It has its roots in satire, stand-up comedy and popular storytelling, where identifying with the part is counterproductive. But its purpose is more analytic, more provocative, more political.

Thus an actor playing Lear should show the character's destructive behaviour as much as the suffering that he experiences. This allows the audience to see that *King Lear* is the tragedy of an entire land, not just a family affair, and understand how the actions of the powerful are responsible for the broader catastrophe. Brecht was clear about what this entailed:

> At no moment must [the actor playing Lear] go so far as to be wholly transformed into the character played. The verdict: 'He didn't act Lear, he was Lear' would be an annihilating blow to him. He has just to show the character, or rather he has to do more than just get into it; this does not mean that if he is playing passionate parts he must remain cold. It is only that his feelings must not at bottom be those of the character, so that the audience's may not at bottom be those of the character either.
>
> *(BoT, 1964, 193–4)*

Similarly, an actor playing the Duke in *Measure for Measure* would find ways of confronting audiences with his character's contradictory values and subject his decisions to public scrutiny. Look at the moment when he announces that he's going to hide from Isabella the fact that her brother Claudio is still alive:

> The tongue of Isabel. She's come to know
> If yet her brother's pardon be come hither,
> But I will keep her ignorant of her good
> To make her heavenly comforts of despair
> When it is least expected.
>
> (4.3.105–9)

Performed with a clear sense that this is a particular decision and that the opposite one could have been taken – what's more, that it is shaped by a particular way of thinking, rich in historical circumstance – will encourage the audience to engage objectively with what the Duke is doing, and not accept his actions at face value. It is as if the audience is being challenged by the actor to criticize and disagree.

Acting with alienation doesn't mean abandoning realistic observation. In fact, rather the opposite: 'The alienation effect does not in any way demand an unnatural way of acting' and 'has nothing whatever to do with ordinary stylization'. Instead, it 'depends on lightness and naturalness of performance' and, above all, critical observation of the world beyond the rehearsal room. For 'when the actor checks the truth of his performance' against 'reality', Brecht explained:

> he is not just thrown back on his 'natural sensibilities', but can always be corrected by a comparison with reality ... He acts in such a way that nearly every sentence could be followed by a verdict of the audience and practically every gesture is submitted for the public's approval.
>
> (BoT, 1964, 95)

Above all, the actor should remain relaxed and alert, lively and bemused, even in the darkest moments:

> It should be apparent all through [his] performance that 'even at the start and in the middle he knows how it ends' and he must 'thus maintain a calm independence throughout.' He narrates the story of his character by vivid portrayal, always knowing more than it does and treating its 'now' and 'here' not as a pretence made possible by the rules of the game, but as something to be distinguished from yesterday and some other place, so as to make visible the knotting together of events.
>
> (BoT, 1964, 194)

Such an approach opens an essential space for independent thought, not just in the actor but in the audience too.

To this end, Brecht sometimes asked his actors to improvise a scene in the third person. The actor playing Hamlet might say,

'Having spoken to a captain of Fortinbras' army to fight for a "little patch of ground / That hath in it no profit the name" Hamlet is forcibly struck by his own failings to carry out revenge, and vows that "from this time forth, / My thoughts be bloody or be nothing worth" (4.4.17-8, 64–5). And, with this, Hamlet's mindset changes.' Such an exercise reminds the actor what it is he is trying to show.

At other times Brecht would ask the actors to read the implied stage directions aloud. Thus, the actor playing Hamlet might say, 'Seeing Claudius at prayer, Hamlet stopped, looked at him and exclaimed suddenly, "Now might I do it"' (*Hamlet*, 3.3.74). Or, the actor playing Benedick might say, 'Having stayed behind in the church to see how Beatrice was holding up, Benedick asked her, "Lady Beatrice, have you wept all this while?"' (*Much Ado*, 4.1.255). This, Brecht explained, 'results in a clash between two tones of voice, alienating the second of them, the text proper':

> Transposing it into the past gives the speaker a standpoint from which he can look back at his sentence. The sentence too is thereby alienated without the speaker adopting an unreal point of view; unlike the spectator, he has read the play right through and is better placed to judge the sentence in accordance with the ending, with its consequences, than the former, who knows less and is more of a stranger to the sentence.
> (*BoT*, 1964, 138)

It's worth experimenting with this, especially because it makes the actor decide on a particular moment of action, and create a visible relationship with the other characters.

The alienation effect emerged, above all, in response to Brecht's dissatisfaction with the way traditional audiences watched plays. Where the bourgeoisie sat in solemn silence, Brecht encouraged laughter and talk, not unlike the atmosphere at the boxing match, the music hall or the circus. He even suggested that smoking should be permitted: 'One lone cigar smoking individual at a performance of Shakespeare would bring about the downfall of all of western art', he declared hyperbolically, adding that it would be impossible 'for an actor to perform in an unnatural, convulsive, and antiquated manner in the presence of a smoker in the pit' (Ewen, 1967, 161).

Thus the alienation effect is fundamental to a kind of theatre whose worth depends on 'the representation of reality with a view to influencing it' (*BoT*, 1964, 225). The problem, Brecht argued, was that 'the theatre as we know it shows the structure of society (represented in the stage) as incapable of being influenced by society (in the auditorium)'. This had to change. The traditional way of reading Shakespeare does the same: his 'great solitary figures, bearing on the breast the star of their fate, carry through with irresistible force their futile and deadly outbursts; they prepare their own downfall; life not death, becomes obscene as they collapse; the catastrophe is beyond criticism. Human sacrifices all round!' Countering this with rational analysis and critical questioning is fundamental: 'We know that the barbarians have their art. Let us create another' (*BoT*, 1964, 189). Above all, Brecht insisted, 'the attitude is a critical one' (*BoT*, 1964, 185).

Indeed, Stanley Mitchell, the poet and eminent scholar of Walter Benjamin, described Brecht's work on Shakespeare as 'experiments in whether a historical event and its literary treatment might be made to turn out differently or at least be viewed differently'. Such an approach, he explained, 'is a deliberate unseating of the supremacy of tragedy and tragic inevitability', and alienation is fundamental to making this happen (Benjamin, 1998, xii). For, as Brecht put it, 'the exposition of the story and its communication by suitable means of alienation constitute the main business of the theatre' (*BoT*, 1964, 202). The essential point, then, is that, when subjected to alienation, the familiar is made strange and the strange rendered familiar. It's the basis for all social change.

Provocations, Exercises and Practical Suggestions

- Choose a scene and see how much can be performed with an eye on the audience. Encourage those watching to be vocal in their objections: 'You can't do that to her!', 'That's not fair', 'Ooh, I wouldn't do that if I was you' and see how the rehearsal room can become a chamber for debate. Encourage the performers to provoke the audience into response. This will be lively and maybe chaotic but revealing too.
- Experiment with prefacing each speech with an 'action' using the third person and set in the past: 'And then he

suggested to her', 'And then he insisted', 'And then she demanded' etc.
- Or simply tell the action of the scene in the past tense: 'The King entered and announced that he wanted to divide his kingdom.' This should be done as an exercise in epic storytelling without using Shakespeare's text at all.

Emotion and Empathy

It's sometimes argued that the Brechtian theatre is fatally lacking in emotion. And done badly, it can feel cold and bloodless. But Brecht's aims were more sophisticated, more human, indeed, than such caricature allows.

Brecht was certainly suspicious of excessive emotionalism, which Stephen Parker attributes to anxiety about his own cardiac function (he died of heart failure at 58). But it should also be seen in the context of his time. Brecht recognized the power of Nazi performative politics (as well as growing tribalism on the left), which relied, above all, on hypnosis, emotional identification and unqualified empathy to make its mark:

> Already in the last years of the Weimar Republic, the post-war German drama took a decisively rationalistic turn. Fascism's grotesque emphasizing of the emotions, together perhaps with the no less important threat to the rational element in Marxist aesthetics, led us to lay particular stress on the rational.
> (*BoT*, 1964, 145)

In other words, an emotional response is not always a good thing.

The insistence on emotion above all was fundamental to the classical theatre of Brecht's youth, which saw empathy as one of its chief effects. Brecht came to understand, however, that such a pursuit was alien to Shakespeare:

> Take the element of conflict in Elizabethan plays, complex, shifting, largely impersonal, never soluble, and then see what has been made of it today, whether in contemporary plays or in contemporary renderings of the Elizabethans. Compare the

part played by empathy then and now. What a contradictory, complicated and intermittent operation it was in Shakespeare's theatre!

(*BoT*, 1964, 161)

'Such a theatre', Brecht concluded, 'appeals less to the feelings than to the spectator's reason', who is, consequently, encouraged to 'come to grips with things' (*BoT*, 1964, 23). Indeed, the Actor in the *Messingkauf* is sceptical about the role of empathy in traditional acting:

> I reckon you've got an exaggerated view – almost an illusion – of how deeply we actors of the old theatre empathize with the characters we play. I can assure you that when we're playing King Lear we're thinking about all kinds of things Lear is very unlikely to have thought about.
>
> (*BoP*, 2014, 101)

In other words, empathy may be a quality more treasured by commentators than by artists and audiences themselves. As Margot Heinemann insists, individual empathy 'is only *one* kind of feeling, and not one that the Shakespearean theatre itself relies on much' (1994, 238).

An example of the misuse of empathy can be seen in the way that Falstaff in the *Henry IV* plays is often performed. Actors try to make him as seductive as possible, a pleasure-seeking alternative to Hal's austerity, a lovable example of flawed humanity who deserves to be celebrated as the sinning Adam who lurks within us all. What such a reading neglects, however, is the evident criminality of his way of life, or how he exploits Mistress Quickly's kindness and Doll Tearsheet's body; it also overlooks his attitude towards his recruits whom he views with downright contempt ('food for powder, food for powder', who will 'fill a pit as well as better', 4.2.64–6). Brecht, I think, would want us to see Falstaff not simply as an old man in physical and mental decline but as a manifestation of the worst elements of a corrupt and decaying ruling elite.

Another example might be Hamlet himself. Thus, Shakespeare's prince is both a sensitive intellectual, hesitating to carry out his dead father's implacable commands, and a young man who is appallingly cruel to Ophelia, careless in his murder of Polonius, merciless in his instructions that his friends, the naïve Rosencrantz and Guildenstern, should be killed and quite capable of bringing about a dreadful bloodbath at the end. Performed well, the audience experiences richly contradictory responses and feels both empathy and distaste, admiration and criticism, joy and dismay – a perfect image of life itself.

A feel for such multiple perspectives is essential: 'It is too great a simplification if we make the actions fit the character and the character fit the actions: the inconsistencies which are to be found in the actions of real people cannot be shown like this' (*BoT*, 1964, 195). In other words, the 'great realist' takes a rounded view of his characters and working only for sympathy runs against the rich grain of the texts. As Brecht wrote about a peasant girl mourning her brother's departure for a 'peasants war' (against the landowners, presumably):

> Are we to surrender to her sorrow completely? Or not at all? We must be able to surrender to her sorrow and at the same time not to. Our actual emotion will come from recognizing and feeling the incident's double aspect.
>
> (*BoT*, 1964, 271)

Real life is more complex than bad art allows. Mere empathy isn't enough.

Provocations, Exercises and Practical Suggestions

- Examine those moments in a Shakespeare play when audiences traditionally empathize with the central character and see how you can make him/her less appealing: e.g. Hamlet in Act Five, or Juliet taking the sleeping drug (4.3).
- Do the opposite with a character we usually despise: e.g., the murderers of Banquo in *Macbeth*, or Don John, Conrade and Borachio in *Much Ado About Nothing*. How can we ask audiences to think more objectively about such figures?
- Experiment with two different performances of Hamlet's famous speech, 'To be or not to be' (3.1.55–87): let the first

strive for sympathy in every way possible, but the second encourage the audience to see him at a greater critical distance (self-indulgent, indecisive, entitled, perhaps?). Do the same with Lady Macbeth's speech, 'The raven himself is hoarse' (1.5.38–58).

- Look at the last moments of your favourite Shakespeare play and discuss how the audience could be encouraged to think more critically. Has order really been restored? Have the bad been punished and the good rewarded? What has changed, and what has stayed the same?

Complex Seeing

A theatre which successfully allies emotion to reason produces in the audience a fundamentally realistic response. Brecht coined the phrase 'complex seeing' to describe the phenomenon whereby we're confronted with a set of opposed perspectives and are asked to observe them dialectically.

Such a technique can be found throughout Shakespeare. A good example is *Antony and Cleopatra*, where, as Harold Bloom writes, 'since no privileged perspective is granted to the audience, the dramatic ironies proliferate and cannot be controlled by us' (Bloom, 1999, 560). Constantly shifting viewpoints demand that we watch the action from a global vantage point: from Rome to Egypt, Parthia to Actium and so on. As the great Edwardian Shakespearean Harley Granville Barker argued, the 'relays of minor characters, each with a life of its own, help keep the play alive' (Granville Barker, 1993, 139). Similarly, in the two parts of *Henry IV*, Shakespeare counterpoints scenes of revelry in the tavern in Eastcheap with the rigours of Westminster, the battlefield at Shrewsbury with the apple orchards of Gloucestershire, in such a way that our appreciation of each changes the way that we view the other, and neither offers the final word.

Small scenes are similarly thick with contrasting perspectives. Look, for example, at a tiny episode in *Macbeth*: Banquo is talking to his son, Fleance and, using a simple domestic image (with its own resonance of disaster), explains why the night is so dark: 'There's husbandry in heaven; / Their candles are all out' (2.1.4–5). There's a paternal tenderness here that the childless Macbeth can only dream of, and we observe the two families in counterpoint to each other.

Or read aloud the scene between Lady Macduff and her son (4.2) and her own desperate rhetorical questioning when advised to leave:

> Whither should I fly?
> I have done no harm. But I remember now
> I am in this earthly world, where, to do harm
> Is often laudable; to do good, sometime
> Accounted dangerous folly: why then, alas!
> Do I put up that womanly defence,
> To say, I have done no harm?
>
> (4.2.73–8)

With its combination of deep feeling, philosophical scepticism and sharp political insight, this could be by Brecht himself, and the Brechtian director will insist that the actress helps the audience understand the limited choices facing her and other victims of persecution. Such a perspective shocks an audience with its candour, and helps us understand that Macbeth's murders of Macduff's 'pretty chickens and their dam' (4.3.218) are morally worse than the political assassination of King Duncan or the fratricidal murder of Banquo: it is the Massacre of the Innocents itself. 'Did Heaven look on, / And would not take their part?' asks Macduff when he hears the news: Hitler's victims asked the same question, and with good reason too.

Provocations, Exercises and Practical Suggestions

- Ask your group to improvise a ten-minute drama about an episode from everyday life (going to the shop to buy milk, meeting a new neighbour, trying to keep a secret etc.) and see how many different perspectives you can create: the shopkeeper is an illegal immigrant, your new neighbour has just been released from gaol, the secret you're being asked to keep is dubious etc. Ensure that each of these is given full voice.

- Take a scene in Shakespeare and see how many contrasting perspectives you can find. Above all, notice how often the actions of the powerful are subjected to criticism and their objectives are frustrated by others. Ask your group to concentrate on these alternative perspectives and see how impassioned, how dignified, how full of life they are, but also how subversive.

Useful Junction Points

Brecht alerted us to what he called 'useful junction points'. These are moments in the text 'where what was new in his age collided with what was old' (*BoP*, 2014, 92). In such places, Brecht insisted, we glimpse how things change.

This can be seen in the first part of *Henry IV* in the conflict between the King's mission of centralizing and consolidating royal powers and the fierce resistance that he encounters from the Percies in Northumberland, Douglas in Scotland and Glendower in Wales. Two world views are in collision with each other.

A more domestic example can be found in *Twelfth Night* in the attitude towards the Puritanism of the steward Malvolio from the alliance of the upwardly mobile servant, Maria, with the two faded aristocrats, Sir Toby Belch and Sir Andrew Aguecheek. Again, the new comes into conflict with the old in rich and revealing ways.

Such historic collisions are evident in more personal places too. Thus, Hermia's defiance of her father in the opening scene of *A Midsummer Night's Dream* is more than merely personal: she is defying the control exerted by the father of an aristocratic young woman in finding her a husband. It's only when we understand that Egeus is simply doing his paternal duty that we see that Hermia is challenging not just her father but the entire status quo. This reaches its dramatic climax in 4.1 when Theseus decides to 'overbear [Egeus'] will'.

Similarly, Leonato's fury with his daughter in *Much Ado* (4.1) when told that she's been unfaithful before her wedding is driven by his own sense of paternal failure. Both fathers have a duty to their daughters to keep them chaste before marriage, and it is ahistorical to think they are simply being cruel. These episodes gain in greater resonance when we recognize that they echo the emergence of new notions of the 'companionate marriage' among the English aristocracy.

Such 'useful junction points' can be discovered wherever we look, once we have learnt to see the plays as dramatizing historic change, not simply expressing psychological or personal crises.

Provocations, Exercises and Practical Suggestions

- Take a Shakespeare play and define the underlying historic conflicts embodied in the action.
- Ask your group to identify specific moments when these forces come into conflict with each other, and explain the nature of that conflict. Thus, when Theseus 'overbears' Egeus, the actor could preface his words in rehearsal by explaining: 'At that moment, the Duke decided to ignore a thousand years of custom and insisted that a young woman should be allowed to choose her husband and not be subject to her father's will.' Such an exercise might help the actor bring out the historical significance of what is happening.

'Words, Words, Words'

Brecht was a magnificent poet, probably the greatest German poet of the twentieth century, even declaring that 'my poetry is the strongest argument against my playwriting activities' (*P*, 1976, x). His English was limited, however, and, in studying Shakespeare, he was fortunate to be helped first by his bilingual collaborator Elisabeth Hauptmann and then the fine English actor Charles Laughton, who read the plays aloud to him in his garden in Santa Monica.

Brecht's views about Elizabethan verse are illuminating. In an early essay he enthusiastically describes 'the greater force of the actors' delivery when they used the almost unreadable "stumbling" verses' of the eighteenth-century translations rather than a 'smooth' new one. And he goes on to explain how in co-translating

Christopher Marlowe's *Edward II* he devised a rhythmic style which had the 'jerky breath of a man running', and embraced the original's eccentricities and particularities. Above all, he wanted the verse to show 'human dealings as contradictory, fiercely fought over, full of violence' (*BoT*, 1964, 115–16).

Thus, the Brechtian actor would do everything he can to resist the blandness of traditional classical speaking and engage, instead, with the bumpy energy that is so fundamental to Shakespeare's language. And this is more than just a question of poetic form: rather, the shifting genres express shifting attitudes, and the play's meaning – such as it can be found – emerges from such contradiction.

Brecht repeatedly called for a poetic language which follows 'the *gest* of the person speaking'. He explained his preference for the biblical phrase, 'If thine eye offends you, pluck it out', to the more passive, 'Pluck out the eye that offends thee', arguing that the first has a visceral energy – 'It is far richer and cleaner from a *gestic* point of view' (*BoT*, 1964, 117) – and a greater dramatic impact. Such qualities are fundamental to Shakespeare's dramatic language and need to be embraced.

Brecht would have relished the juxtaposition of the Anglo-Saxon and the Romance in Shakespeare. A famous example can be found in *Macbeth*:

> Will all great Neptune's ocean wash this blood
> Clean from my hand? No, this my hand will rather
> The multitudinous seas incarnadine,
> Making the green one red.
>
> (2.2.59–62)

The Brechtian actor would contrast the Latinism of 'multitudinous seas incarnadine' with the Anglo-Saxon power of 'making the green one red', and let the two play off against each other. Something similar can be seen when Macduff hears of the murder of his wife and children. The young Malcolm advises Macduff to 'make us med'cines of our great revenge, / To cure this deadly grief' (4.3.214–5) but first, as Macduff declares (and Brecht would surely endorse), he must first 'feel it as a man' (4.3.221). And then, in a moment of peculiarly Shakespearean genius, he resorts to farmyard imagery to express his loss:

What, all my pretty chickens, and their dam,
At one fell swoop?

(4.3.218-9)

And it this domestic everyday language which never fails to move an audience to tears: tears of grief, yes, but also tears of rage at what Macbeth has done. Elevated language is 'alienated' by a more direct register, and both are granted power and resonance. The educated teach the uneducated and, crucially, the other way round.

Punctuation can have an impact. When I direct Shakespeare, I create a new edition of the play. Drawing on a wide range of academic editions, as well as the Folio and the Quartos, these are very lightly punctuated, with no colons, semi-colons or exclamation marks, and as few commas as I can get away with (and never at the end of a verse line). This, I believe, encourages a kind of speaking with its own dynamic energy.

Thus, in *Hamlet*, I prefer 'O what a noble mind is here overthrown' to 'Oh! What a noble mind is here o'erthrown!' The first offers a simple expression of despair: the second, an editorial intervention. Such orthographic simplicity helps the actor to speak the text with the *gestic* energy that Brecht would have wanted and reminds him that the published elisions are simply indicators of rhythm (it is, I believe, possible to say the word 'overthrown' with the 'v' included in the diphthong in 'o'erthrown'). It also provides for an immediate alienation effect which encourages the actor to think for himself.

Finally, Brecht wanted the actor to be alert to the opportunities for direct address. This doesn't just mean the soliloquies, where an open-hearted relationship with the audience is often revealing, but also in the middle of a scene where the actor can turn to the audience to enlist support. This is much easier on the Elizabethan stage where the actor can engage directly with the public without interrupting the forward movement of the action. Indeed, direct address, the knowing complicity between actor and audience, is fundamental to Brecht's entire project. Done well, it engages the interest of everyone in the theatre – a political act in its own right.

Words matters, and how they are delivered is critical for a political, social approach to Shakespeare, that most verbal of playwrights. What's more, as the mighty civil rights activist, playwright and novelist, James Baldwin, memorably declared, 'The greatest poet in the English language found his poetry where poetry is found: in the lives of the people' (Baldwin, 1964, 65–9). It's an insight we forget at our peril.

Provocations, Exercises and Practical Suggestions

- Type up a Shakespeare speech and remove all the punctuation. Ask the actor to reintroduce a handful of full stops, commas and question marks, to indicate the basic structures of the sentences, but nothing more and don't use commas at the end of a verse line. What effect does this have?
- If anyone in your group speaks a foreign language, find an unfamiliar translated speech, and, without saying where the speech comes from, ask him/her to translate it back into English. Then compare it to the original. The aim is to sense the potential of Shakespeare in translation, but also the visceral power of the original.

3

Staging

There comes a day when rehearsals end and the production moves on to the stage. This, as any director knows, is the moment of truth, when the real challenges of the live theatre assert themselves. And it's when the many thoughts about design, lighting, music and staging are tested to destruction.

The Lessons of the Globe

Despite his interest in history, Brecht's Shakespeare was the opposite of 'museum theatre'.

As a dedicated materialist, he was keen to understand the physical conditions of the Elizabethan playhouse. 'In the last two decades of his life', David Barnett explains, 'Brecht signalled a desire to learn as much as possible about Shakespeare and the Globe', and while his views were 'hopelessly mired in the scholarship of the 1920s and 1930s', his underlying conclusions are borne out by modern academic study (2013, 124).

The Elizabethan theatre, Brecht realized, consisted of a non-illusory stage surrounded on three sides by a diverse audience with whom the carefully delineated and three-dimensional characters enjoyed a direct relationship. On this platform, Brecht recognized, Shakespeare's company enacted compelling stories of political struggle and social upheaval. And catering for as many as 3000 people, and positioned on the edge of the rapidly expanding capital, he understood that the amphitheatres on the South Bank of the

Thames offered a perfect forum for large-scale debates about the way society works, and how the future should unfold. It is only by sensing something of this context, both social and cultural, theatrical and political, Brecht knew, that we can grasp the scale of this astonishing moment in dramatic history, and discover our own way of staging the plays today.

Brecht admired, above all, the simplicity of the Elizabethan theatre and, responding to Goethe's despair at its 'inadequacy', was typically brisk:

> 'Aids to naturalness' have led to such emphasis being put on illusion that we newcomers would sooner think of Shakespeare on an empty stage than a Shakespeare who had ceased to stimulate or provoke any use of the imagination.
>
> (*BoT*, 1964, 218)

He was particularly struck by the way that the Elizabethan stage deployed minimal suggestion of place:

> If you are also aware that they performed (and also rehearsed, of course!) by daylight in the open air, mostly without any attempt to indicate the location of the action and in close proximity to the spectators, who sat all the way round the stage as well as on it, while quite a few of them were standing up or walked around – then you begin to get a good idea of how earthly, profane and unmagical it all was.
>
> (*BoP*, 2014, 55–6)

Indeed, he declared, the 'restoration of the theatre's reality as theatre is a precondition for any realistic representation of how people live together':

> Too much heightening of the illusion in the setting, along with a 'magnetic' manner of acting which gives the spectator the illusion of being present at a fleeting, fortuitous, 'real' event, create such an impression of naturalness that we can no longer interpose our own judgement, imagination or reactions, and must simply conform by sharing in the experience and becoming one of nature's objects.
>
> (*BoP*, 2014, 186–7)

Such a stage, Brecht knew, required the willing suspension of our disbelief – the *active* suspension, one might say. Thus, the Chorus in *Henry V* begs the audience to let our 'imaginary forces work' (Prol.18), while Theseus in *A Midsummer Night's Dream* consoles the onstage audience with the notion that even the worst acting is forgivable if 'simpleness and duty tender it' (5.1.83). As Brecht insisted, 'people were expected to use their imaginations' (*BoP*, 2014, 56).

Typically, however, Brecht saw the working of the imagination in political terms: that is, by presenting dramatic scenarios in a provisional fashion, the audience sees the world as similarly needing improvement. And so, our 'imaginary forces' are more than mere neurological phenomena; their deployment is the prerequisite to social change. Above all, as Brecht argued:

> The illusion created by the theatre must be a partial one, so that it can always be recognized as illusion. Reality, however completely represented, must be altered by art, so that it may be seen to be subject to change and treated as such.
>
> (*BoP*, 2014, 187)

Fighting for a 'better world than this' (*As You Like It*, 1.2.273) is the point, not rediscovering how to play like a child.

Provocations, Exercises and Practical Suggestions

- Choose a scene from Shakespeare and consider staging it without electric lights or sound, using just two doors, a throne and a handful of props.
- Explore how short the gaps between the scenes can be under these conditions and think how this confronts the audience with contradictory images, voices and content.
- Listen for how Shakespeare gives all the information needed about the location, but also when it is simply irrelevant.
- Consider the way the actors can best solicit the audience for their opinions. Look for opportunities for direct address, not unlike a barrister appealing to the jury.
- How might this affect the nature of the debate the actor can enjoy with the audience?

Stage Design

When a modern production of Shakespeare is described as 'Brechtian', it usually refers to its stage design, especially if it has explicit political content.

What is striking, however, in the work of Brecht's great designers (or 'scenographers') – Caspar Neher, Karl von Appen and Teo Otto – is how simple their work was, how understated. They often employed a pure white cyclorama, with occasional flying or freestanding pieces of naturalistic scenery, suggesting doors, parts of walls or even, as in *Mother Courage*, a roof. These, then, along with carefully selected costumes, props and furniture, created a sequence of fast-moving images, often reminiscent of classical or biblical iconography, frequently interrupted by a white half curtain running across the front.

Brecht's description of Neher's 'masterful' approach is revealing:

> [His] sets are significant statements about reality. He takes a bold sweep, never letting inessential detail or decoration distract from the statement, which is an artistic and an intellectual one. At the same time everything has beauty, and the essential detail is most lovingly carried out.
>
> (*BoT*, 1964, 231)

Something similar can be seen in von Appen's designs for Brecht's *Coriolan* in 1964: a simple white cyclorama and a pale floor created an abstract space, but at the centre of the revolving stage stood a large gateway with a section of wall suggesting Rome on one side and Corioles on the other (photos of several of these can be found on the Getty Images website, or the *Coriolan Modellbuch*, 1964). Against this, the figures with their suggestive weapons, siege ladders and heavy armour, were vividly positioned and their relationships made clear:

> Some of the most imaginative bits of staging in *Coriolanus* involve the use of the revolving stage which, instead of being a conventional device for simplifying the shifting of scenery, becomes an eloquent interpretive tool.
>
> (*TDR*, 1967, 113)

And when pressed on the 'inauthenticity' of the production's props and costumes, co-director Joachim Tenschert was frank:

> No, our work was based in very extensive research, but the research was not confined to the period in which the play takes place.
>
> (*TDR*, 1967, 113)

Such approximation is fundamental to the Brechtian aesthetic, where the visual information suggests what the world of the play might look like, but encourages the audience to fill in the rest. As the American father of Method acting, Lee Strasberg commented admiringly: 'There is no attempt at completeness in the physical staging, which consists entirely of selected details' (Barnett, 2015b, 32). And such incompleteness encourages the audience to watch the action in all its consequences, and see how better solutions could have been arrived at.

It's important to emphasize, however, that Brecht wasn't striving for mere abstraction. Indeed, he declared, 'stylization should not remove the natural element but should heighten it' (*BoT*, 1964, 204). Instead, he 'based his realism on a materialist view of the world and insisted that everything on stage had material causes' (Barnett, 2015b, 60). He knew that meaning in the theatre is best understood by watching human beings in relationship to inanimate objects, be it the 'chalk circle' from which the child is torn, Mother Courage dragging her tatty cart against the revolve, or Galileo using an apple to teach a young boy about the movements of the heavenly bodies. And he painted Hegel's maxim that 'the truth is concrete' in large letters on a beam over his desk: for it is in material objects that meaning can be found.

Similarly, in Shakespeare, meaning is generated by characters interacting with emblematic objects: the deposed king confronted by the cracked mirror in *Richard II* (4.1), the young prince examining the grinning features of a skull in *Hamlet* (5.1.174–85), Falstaff being thrown into the Thames from a basket of dirty laundry in *The Merry Wives of Windsor* (3.3) or Malcolm's soldiers advancing behind the green leaves of Birnam Wood in *Macbeth* (5.6). Such material objects make abstract ideas tangible, and with them the word becomes flesh. As such they deserve to be lovingly prepared: for, in the hands of the 'great realist', they are the chief object of the audience's attention.

Importantly, creating such simple beauty doesn't have to be extravagant, as Brecht described in a late poem:

> The decors and costume of the great Neher
> Are made of cheap material.
> Out of wood, rags and colour
> He makes the Basque fisherman's hovel
> And imperial Rome.
>
> (P, 1976, 429)

It's a useful lesson for the cash-strapped theatre of today.

Provocations, Exercises and Practical Suggestions

- Look at the opening of *The Tempest* (1.1) or the long scene in the woods outside Athens in *A Midsummer Night's Dream* (3.2), and experiment with staging them with just two chairs, simple white lighting, no scenery and sound effects created by banging on a steel bucket.
- Stage the first scene of *King Lear* using only a throne, a crown and a paper map. What is gained? What is lost?
- Place a key prop (a skull, a bottle of wine, a pair of boots) in an empty space and see how it gains in focus and emblematic meaning. Stage a scene in which that prop is at the heart of the dramatic impact: for example, a man lost in a jungle discovering that his mobile phone has run out of power, or a woman trying to get a second box of food from the food bank for her child. See how objects are at the heart of good political drama.
- Similarly, see how the struggle for power in a Shakespeare play is heightened if there is only one chair used in the action: the throne itself, then, becomes the embodiment of power.

Arrangements and Blocking

The good designer, Brecht explained, 'always starts with "the people themselves" and "what is happening to or through them." He provides no "décor", frames and backgrounds, but constructs the space for "people" to experience something in' (*BoT*, 1964, 231–2). On such a stage, the visual impact lies in the disposition of the figures themselves, and the Brechtian theatre uses blocking to articulate changing social relationships as vividly as possible: 'The grouping of the characters ... and the movements of the groups must be such that the necessary beauty is attained above all by the elegance with which the material conveying that *gest* is set out and laid bare to the understanding of the audience' (*BoT*, 1964, 200–1).

Such groupings should be laden with gestic meaning. We should be able to see how the courtiers abase themselves in the presence of the king even as they are plotting to replace him, how the nobility treats the people who work for them with a mixture of indulgence and contempt, and the brutal actions the gentry take to face down the peasantry. Critically, such relationships should be physicalized in such a way that they can be easily understood, and with such style that they are pleasurable to watch.

In Brecht, as in Shakespeare, a relatively small group of actors are used to represent crowds, and audiences are expected to read the action both metaphorically and literally, imaginatively and figuratively. Furthermore, the actors employ a repertoire of readily understood gestures and postures, and the result is a continuously evolving pictogram appealing to the eyes as much as to the ears, to aesthetic appreciation as much as to political insight. And so, we enjoy watching the proud ruler clinging desperately onto his throne, the servants huddled together doing what they can do to oppose injustice, and the gentry flaunting their wealth in such a way that it seems to be their natural right. Understanding and enjoyment go hand in hand.

In summary, Brecht wanted each episode to be presented as an artefact, intact for a moment before dissolving into a new one, suggesting that social structures are likewise impermanent and capable of being changed.

Provocations, Exercises and Practical Suggestions

- Take a figurative classical painting (for example Piero della Francesca's 'Resurrection of Christ' or Géricault's 'Raft of the Medusa') and reproduce as accurately as you can the physical relationships.
- Using a similar technique tell the story of a scene in Shakespeare with (perhaps) ten simple arrangements of an arrangement of bodies frozen in time, in mid gesture. Take photographs of each and discuss how the dramatic interplay could be altered to have a more meaningful impact.
- Place your group in a cluster facing one member standing alone. What kind of story does this suggest? And how does a small adjustment (introducing a pointed finger, a back turned, a wicked smile etc.) change the meaning of what is being shown?

Costumes and Clothes

Brecht understood that for all its bare-board simplicity, the Shakespearean stage was a powerfully visual art form.

This was partly a consequence of the Globe's highly decorated (and metaphorically conceived) pillars, tiring house and canopy, but more because of the impact of the figures themselves. The costumes worn by the rich and powerful were often lavish (frequently donated by real nobility) and the working people (regardless of period) wore the same clothes as their brothers and sisters in the audience. Thus, in a time when laws strictly stipulated what clothes could be worn by social rank, costumes clarified status and power relations. Kings and nobility, but also prelates, justices and men at arms, weren't just powerful, they had to look powerful. Clothes communicated a huge amount, onstage as in the streets.

In the modern theatre, costuming is a more self-conscious affair, and the director and designer are involved in a series of decisions about costuming as they develop a physical form to illuminate the director's *fabel*. Brecht knew that this was a complicated matter and described how in the Weimar theatre 'Shakespeare was frequently refashioned and changed':

> There were so many interpretations extracted from the classical works that they hardly had any left in them. We saw Hamlet in a dinner jacket, Caesar in a uniform, and at least the dinner jacket and uniform profited by it and gained respectability. The experiments are very uneven, and the most remarkable ones are not always the most worthwhile, but even the most worthless are scarcely ever completely worthless. As far as Hamlet in a dinner jacket is concerned, that is hardly more of a sacrilege for Shakespeare than the conventional Hamlet in silk tights.
>
> (*BoT*, 2015, 158)

Crucially, Brecht concluded, 'Both remain within the framework of the costume play'. In other words, decisions about costumes are political and deserve careful thought.

We should also remember that Shakespeare has always been performed in modern dress: a sketch of a performance of *Titus Andronicus* shows an intriguing combination of Elizabethan clothes and Roman togas. And the great English director and playwright Harley Granville Barker introduced dinner jackets in his Shakespeare seasons at the Savoy before the First World War. In other words modern dress doesn't *necessarily* confer modern understanding, just as historical costumes are only effective if accompanied by historical – and political – insight.

Provocations, Exercises and Practical Suggestions

- In Shakespeare's England, working people wore naturally toned clothes, while the aristocracy sported dyed fabrics, often black, with embroidery, jewellery, daggers and so on. Explore the way that these contrasting tones communicate contrasting classes. Look, for example, at the scene (4.7) in *Henry VI Part 2* when Jack Cade and his followers – all dressed in various shades of brown and grey – are confronted by the magnificently apparelled Duke of Buckingham and Old Lord Clifford.

- Consider what is needed to indicate the clothes worn in ancient Rome for *Julius Caesar* or *Coriolanus*. If togas are to be avoided, how can we suggest the world of the play? What happens when the characters are all dressed in modern business suits? What is lost, but what is gained?

Lighting and Signs

With his insistence on contrasting perspectives, Brecht wanted everything on stage to be granted equal status, and (literally) no one left in the dark. To this end, he asked for simple white lighting with minimal shifts of intensity, and used none of the lighting designer's usual tricks to create atmosphere. Indeed, in response to the Actor's anxiety that *A Midsummer Night's Dream* would be 'performed in daylight' and that 'it was daylight when the ghost appeared in *Hamlet*?' Brecht's Dramaturg is direct: 'People were expected to use their imaginations' (*BoP*, 2014, 56).

Brecht's poem 'The Lighting' explained his thinking:

> Give us some light on the stage, electrician. How can we
> Playwrights and actors put forward
> Our images of the world in half-darkness?
>
> (*P*, 1976, 426)

Brecht also insisted that the audience should be able to see the lamps and cables – 'No one would expect the lighting to be hidden at a sporting event, a boxing match, for instance' (*BoT*, 1964, 141) – as part of the broader demystification of cultural production. And, as with Shakespeare, the musicians played in full view of the audience. In other words, this was a theatre committed to clarity and had nothing hidden up its sleeves.

One of Brecht's most recognized innovations was 'the literalization of the theatre', the use of text in stage design. This can be seen in the location signs hanging over the action in *Mother Courage* or the words displayed behind the actors in the *lehrstücke*. There is no evidence to suggest that the King's Men used anything similar, but the framing which is such a feature of the Globe – the stage as the earth, hell beneath the trapdoor and the painted heavens above – was rich with metaphorical meaning. The neo-classical *theatrum mundi* (in which 'all the world is a stage') encouraged audiences to see the action as a self-conscious representation of real life, not mere escapism. Such literalization (perhaps using projection) could be of use in modern productions of Shakespeare, especially those plays which rely on extensive prior historical knowledge.

Provocations, Exercises and Practical Suggestions

- Explore a night scene in Shakespeare (the wood in *A Midsummer Night's Dream*, perhaps) and see what happens when it is played in open white light. How will the audience know when it is taking place? Likewise the storm in *King Lear*?
- Devise a series of projections which can help the audience understand the political backstory of one of the history plays.

Speed, Pleasure and Fun

One of the striking things about the 1957 film of the stage production of *Mother Courage* is the speed of the speaking, the lightness of touch and the sense of energy that radiates off the stage. The world that is being dramatized may be challenging, but the actors of the Berliner Ensemble presented people engaging with its realities in the liveliest way imaginable: cracking jokes, talking with – and at – each other, and taking pleasures wherever they could be found.

Of course we have to be careful: pace in the theatre consists of more than just speaking quickly and with high spirits. And Brecht insisted that his actors should 'play one thing after another', eager that the audience should be able to follow every moment of choice, however trivial, however nuanced. But his emphasis on clarity, precision and edge means that theatrical attack – Hamlet's instruction to speak the speech 'trippingly on the tongue' (3.2.2) – was fundamental.

Furthermore, Brecht argued, the 'playing should be infused with the *gest* of handing over a finished article. What now comes before the spectator is the most frequently repeated of what has not been rejected and so the finished representations have to be delivered with the eyes fully open, so that they may be received with the eyes open too' (*BoT*, 1964, 204). Such controlled energy, such mastery of the material, such alienation in the acting is essential, as can be sensed from an instruction about the performance of his adaptation of *Measure for Measure*: '[It] has to be played with complete seriousness in the heightened and impassioned style of the Elizabethan theatre' (*BoT*, 1964, 101–2).

Indeed, just nine days before he died, Brecht sent a message to his actors on the eve of their triumphant London season. Acknowledging that in England there is a 'long standing fear that German art must be terribly heavy, slow, laborious and pedestrian', he insisted that their playing should be 'quick, light, strong':

> This is not a question of hurry, but of speed, not simply of quick playing, but of quick thinking... In the dialogues the exchanges must not be offered reluctantly, as when offering somebody one's last pair of boots, but must be tossed like so many balls. The audience has to see that here are a number of artists working together as an ensemble in order to convey stories, ideas, virtuoso feats to the spectator by a common effort.
>
> (*BoT*, 1964, 283)

This offers the ideal antidote to the yawn that so often greets sluggish modern productions of Shakespeare. The phrase, the 'two hours traffic of our stage' (*Romeo and Juliet*, Pro. 12) suggests that the plays were originally presented at speed, with substantial cuts and no lengthy scene changes or musical interludes.

'Giving pleasure', Brecht declared, 'is the noblest function that we have found for "theatre"' (*BoT*, 1964, 180) for, as Elisabeth Hauptmann tells us, Brecht believed Shakespeare 'wrote things primarily that he and his friends got fun out of' (*BoT*, 1964, 9n). Certainly, an infectious sense of enjoyment is essential, and relaxation, ease and high spirits encourage critical oversight and independent thought: 'Let us therefore cause general dismay by revoking our decision to emigrate from the realm of the merely enjoyable, and even more general dismay by announcing our decision to take up lodging there' (*BoT*, 1954, 180). 'Nothing is funnier', Brecht declared, 'than the serious way our theatres perform Shakespeare', who 'may be theatrical, but is never ceremonious'; indeed, 'our philistines are unable to contemplate naivety and complicity together' (*J*, 1993, 118). Above all, he concluded triumphantly, 'Nothing needs less justification than pleasure' (*BoT*, 1964, 181).

Irony is perhaps Brecht's most readily used comic technique: 'Happy the land that has no need of heroes' is Galileo's brilliant response to his pupil's delight in 'the land that has such heroes', and it is with grim irony that Brecht has Mother Courage and the prostitute Yvette delighted to hear that war has broken out again: it'll provide more customers. Shakespeare uses such irony sparingly, but it can be part of the director's toolkit, showing up, for instance, how Jack Cade's aristocratic opponents threaten similar levels of violence that he and his followers offer them; or, in a different key, the way the steward Malvolio in *Twelfth Night* is mocked and persecuted simply for wanting to do better in the world.

A sense of humour is, of course, fundamental to Shakespeare, and Brecht wanted us to embrace it eagerly, especially satirical or subversive humour directed at the powerful. What he wouldn't have enjoyed is the kind of acting which gets its laughs by mocking the 'poor naked wretches' (*King Lear*, 3.4.28). We've all seen such performances – sometimes wrongly defended as being part of a popular tradition – that immediately identify the working people as objects of derision: Brecht knew that the theatre (and the world) deserves better.

Instead, as is quickly evident, the working people are bemused by the pretentions, irrationality and self-indulgence of their betters and joke grimly about their own predicament. Look for example at the messenger who brings Cleopatra the unwelcome news of Antony's marriage to Octavia: in a brilliant scene (2.5.23–74, 84–106), Shakespeare shows the emotional insecurity of a powerful woman in the way that she treats those who are dependent on her favour. If it makes us laugh, it is because of its astonishing realism.

Thus, Brecht argued, pleasure, laughter and devastating irony reveal the complicated truths of the world. It's certainly fundamental to staging Shakespeare in the true Brechtian spirit.

Provocations, Exercises and Practical Suggestions

- Rehearse a scene in Shakespeare and ensure that there are no pauses. Ensure that the speaking is driven, conversational and fluent, and resist the overemphatic broken-up style which sometimes mars modern Shakespearean acting.
- Ask your actors to play a scene with hardly any vocal power, just muttering the lines, but expressing what is happening through their physical relationships. See how this helps them interact with each other in a way that an audience will be able to observe in three dimensions.
- Try the opposite: rehearse a scene with the actors sitting down at a table speaking into microphones but with no eye contact or physical connection. This encourages the actors to concentrate on the sound of the words, on the musicality of the writing (in all its bumpiness), on the way that the language suggests actions in their own right.

How Radical Was Brecht's Approach?

As early as 1927, Brecht insisted that the 'radical transformation of the theatre' had to 'correspond to the whole radical transformation of the mentality of our time' (*BoT*, 1964, 23). Whether he achieved that is beyond the reach of this book, but we can legitimately ask whether he refashioned the plays of the mighty Shakespeare for the modern world? Or did he, rather, just help us see them as the best social and political dramas of their time? In other words how radical was Brecht's approach to Shakespeare?

It is evident that Brecht was not interested in a postmodern assault on the status quo, the dramatic equivalent of painting a red nose on the 'Mona Lisa'. Indeed, such self-conscious postmodern practice was alien to his mature purposes, and can hardly be claimed as Brechtian. But he knew that the dominant way of doing Shakespeare – whether conventionally historicist or modishly expressionist – was not fit for purpose, partly because it didn't engage with contemporary experience but also because it ignored the inherently dialectical qualities of the plays themselves. What was needed, instead, was an approach which challenged audiences to watch the action more critically, while also bringing them closer to the living qualities of the original texts.

In evaluating Brecht's achievements, it's worth starting by considering the extent to which the modern classical theatre has absorbed his thinking. Certainly, wherever we look we see the outward features of the Brechtian theatre: exposed lighting, interposed songs, suggestive scenography, historical approximation, direct address, an ensemble of actors working together to tell the story and so on. The problem is that these are rarely allied to a social or political analysis, let alone a coherent *fabel*. More Brechtian are the many attempts to engage with the 'barbarism' latent within the texts – the racism, sexism, ableism and the rest – which are to be welcomed, even if they are little more than provocative.

We should also consider whether more traditional theatrical methods can take us to the same place. Thus, to take an example from classical German drama, when Brecht took over directing responsibilities on Heinrich von Kleist's *The Broken Jug* at the Berliner Ensemble, his 'concern for detail in class relations meant that hierarchies became clearer than in [a] more psychological approach to the play as a character drama: Walter, the visiting legal official has power over the local judge Adam, but this power cannot be used to undermine Adam before those of a lower class whom he has to judge' (Barnett, 2015b, 108). Now, I've directed Kleist's great comedy, and I know that the original text delivers *exactly* what Brecht emphasized: that is, Walter does everything he can to protect Adam's status as a judge right up to the very last moment. The bigger question, the genuinely Brechtian question, is whether we ought to adjust the play's ending to ensure that the unmasking of a corrupt judge results in something more than simply the imposition of a new – perhaps equally corrupt, probably more punitive – judicial order, aided and abetted by the middle classes against the peasantry. In other words, a careful psychological approach takes us a long way towards Brecht's goals, but the true Brechtian insists that such a reordering – of both text and the world – should include the interests of working people themselves.

In considering modern productions of classical drama hailed as 'radical', we should, I think, be cautious. Indeed, in one of his more abrasive late essays, Brecht described attempts to counter what he called 'the ghastly boredom of traditional productions':

> Actors and producers, many of them talented, set out to remedy this by thinking up new and hitherto unknown sensational effects, which are, however, of a purely formalist kind; that is to say, they are forcibly imposed on the work, on its content and on its message, so that even worse damage results than with traditional-style productions, for in this case message and content are not merely dulled or flattened out but absolutely distorted. Formalist revival of the classics is the answer to stuffy tradition, and it is the wrong one. It is as if a piece of meat had gone off and were only made palatable by saucing and spicing it up.
>
> (*BoT*, 1964, 272)

This critique offers an important challenge, and the Shakespearean director needs to work out where they stand in relationship to it.

Brecht's argument is that it's not good enough to put the play into fancy dress, however chic, however modish, however modern: instead, we should engage with the drama itself, its story, and the conflicts and change that it describes. Indeed, as he warned so powerfully in relation to the Nazis: 'To want the new is old-fashioned, what is new is to want the old' (*J*, 1993, 108). In a time of bewildering innovation, often with troubling consequences, such caution is valid.

Something similar can be observed in Brecht's adoption of aspects of 'Socialist Realism', the official aesthetic of the DDR, whose 'performance of old classical works', he wrote, 'is based on the view that mankind has preserved those works which gave artistic expression to advances towards a continually bolder and more delicate humanity' (*BoT*, 1964, 269n). Of course, emerging out of the catastrophe of National Socialism, Brecht's vision was largely of economic and social justice and what is meant by a 'more delicate humanity' constantly evolves. Furthermore, other questions – gender, race and ethnicity, as well as disabled bodies and minds and the disaster of climate change – preoccupy many today, and a Brechtian response to Shakespeare would need to explore the productive contradictions in these areas too. But the underlying questions of class and inequality are still everywhere to be seen and we cannot work within the Brechtian frame of reference if we simply ignore them. Certainly, in a time when capitalism is failing to deliver on its promise of prosperity for all and societies even as wealthy as Britain are riven by poverty, inequality and despair, the time has surely come for the classical theatre to re-engage with these fundamental concerns.

Brecht's aims were eloquently put: 'The old works have their own values, their own differentiation, their own scale of beauty and truth. Those are what need to be uncovered' (Barnett, 2013, 124). This is certainly a more modest ambition than turning the plays on their heads. Nevertheless, Brecht's lifelong struggle with a moribund and apolitical tradition can help us develop our own politically engaged, socially inclusive approach to Shakespeare which, in turn, can help shed light on our own 'dark times'.

It's quite a challenge, but it must be possible.

Provocations, Exercises and Practical Suggestions

- Discuss with your group what the word 'radical' means in relationship to Shakespeare? Let your answer refer to the telling of the story, not the set and costumes.
- Ask your group to read Brecht's late essay 'Classical Status as an Inhibiting Factor' (*BoT*, 1964, 272–3). Experiment with one actor reading it aloud, and a second providing a critical response after each sentence. In other words, how much does your group agree with Brecht's argument? Disagreement should be encouraged.
- Modern audiences are often troubled by theatrical innovation: modern costumes, video projections, diverse casting, amplified music and so on. Ask your group to imagine the five most common objections ('It's nothing to do with Shakespeare', 'It's just trendy', 'It's ugly' etc.) and devise a short manifesto which offers a clear reason for the innovations that you admire. Improvise a presentation of this manifesto to an imaginary 'conservative' audience member, or to someone coming to see the play for the first time.

- Discuss Brecht's statement that 'The old works have their own values, their own differentiation, their own scale of beauty and truth. Those are what need to be uncovered.' Is this useful for the modern Shakespearean theatre, or would you prefer something more radical, more edgy? And if so, what might that be?

PART THREE

Six Plays

Six Plays

The time has come to consider how we can apply Brecht's thinking to six very different plays.

These have been chosen to represent six distinct phases in Shakespeare's career: the early history play, *Richard III*; the great Elizabethan comedy, *As You Like It*; the definitive 'problem play', *Measure for Measure*; the mighty Jacobean tragedy, *King Lear*; the late political Roman drama, *Coriolanus*; and the mystical romance, *The Tempest*. All six could, in their different ways, benefit from a Brechtian approach and what follows suggests what that might entail.

To do this I will need to explore Brecht's adaptations of two of the plays and scour his writings for whatever specific comments I can find about all of them. But I'll also have to resort to speculation, some of which will be supported by Brecht's theatrical practice, but much of which will require my own practical experience and imaginative understanding.

Although I will refer to many of the key terms of the Brechtian theatre, much of what follows is a direct engagement with the texts themselves. I will regularly 'alienate' characters and events, and occasionally explore the 'barbarism' innate in the writing; I'll draw attention to the 'epic' quality of the storytelling and point to those 'useful junction points' where the historical conflict is made clear. I'll also make suggestions about how the plays can be staged in the Brechtian spirit. Above all, I'll explore those places where the 'dialectic' is most deeply embodied and point to its many 'contradictions'. The emphasis will, for the most part, be on how Brecht helps us read the plays themselves rather than providing a simple blueprint for theatrical production. But, as I hope the book has shown, a Brechtian reading of the play provides the best advice on how to stage it in the Brechtian spirit.

What follows is invariably suggestive and every director, actor, reader and teacher will pursue their own intrigue. But it does come from a deep immersion in Brecht and Shakespeare and will, I hope, spark fresh ideas and new approaches.

Richard III

Arturo Ui and Shakespeare

It was perhaps inevitable that Brecht would be drawn to Shakespeare's account of the rise and fall of a murderous leader. This, after all, offered him a useful mirror to his own 'dark times'. Indeed, *Richard III* is probably the biggest single influence on Brecht's great political satire, *The Resistible Rise of Arturo Ui*, which, he insisted, should be played 'in the grand style ... preferably with obvious harkbacks to the Elizabethan theatre' (*CP*, 1981, 105). Looking at *Richard III* through the lens of *Arturo Ui* we can glimpse more of Brecht's thinking about Shakespeare, as well as Shakespeare's influence on his own work.

In writing *Arturo Ui*, Brecht knew that it wasn't enough to explain the rise of the 'great dictator' in parable form, he had to show what it would take to oppose him: in other words, Ui's rise to be power had to be shown to be 'resistible'. Similarly, if *Richard III* is to be politically meaningful, audiences must acknowledge the central character's charismatic appeal, while also tracking the forces that eventually bring him down. Brecht's deliberate substitution of 'resistible' for the customary 'irresistible' casts light on Shakespeare's original and, just as Brecht refused to present Hitler's rise to power as a natural phenomenon, so the director of *Richard III* should pay as much attention to the forces that oppose Richard as to the tyrant himself.

Brecht described Shakespeare's Richard as a 'dislikeable man who becomes a terrible one', and fundamental to a Brechtian production would be a demonstration of this gradual process of moral degradation. The audience should watch Richard progressing by a carefully calibrated combination of manufactured popular appeal and increasingly unrestrained violence. The director should show this journey in detail, focusing on each step that Richard takes, along with every step that others take to enable him. In this way, audiences will be able to grasp that Richard's seizure of power is the result of specific actions, and not an inevitability.

Brecht was fascinated by the theatricality of populist politics (he described the Nuremberg rallies as impressive theatre), and while there is no direct parallel to the marvellous scene (6) in *Arturo Ui* when the Shakespearean actor teaches the gangster how to deploy rhetoric effectively, the director of *Richard III* would want to show just how carefully manufactured is Richard's demagoguery. Indeed, something of this is evident in the scene (3.5) in which the Duke of Buckingham answers Richard's inquiries about his acting abilities:

> Tut, I can counterfeit the deep tragedian,
> Speak, and look back, and pry on every side,
> Tremble and start at wagging of a straw,
> Intending deep suspicion. Ghastly looks
> Are at my service, like enforced smiles,
> And both are ready in their offices,
> At any time to grace my stratagems.
>
> (3.5.5–11)

As we know from our own times, a successful career in politics requires the performance of feeling, however false, and the Brechtian director would want to expose this.

There are, of course, substantial differences between the two plays, as David Barnett makes clear:

> Ui, unlike Richard, is not driven by his own ambition or lust for power; our first sight of him shows a gangster fallen on hard times, powerless and out of favour. It is the Cabbage Trust who employs him as hired muscle that spurs Ui on initially; he is given a task which then grows until he himself calls the shots later in the play. In a similar constructive vein, in the wooing of Betty Dullfeet, Ui denies the murder of her husband, unlike Richard, and does not seek marriage but access to lucrative markets in Betty's city, a merger of a different sort.
>
> (2013, 136)

Furthermore, *Arturo Ui* is not entirely successful: indeed, the great critic Theodor Adorno argued that Brecht's use of ridicule rendered fascism 'innocuous' and that for the sake of 'political commitment, political reality was trivialized' (Jameson, 1977, 204–5). It's quite a charge, but one which Shakespeare, for all his deployment of Richard's strange charm, brilliantly avoids.

What Ui and Richard have in common is a potent mixture of theatrical energy and psychological intuition, personal despair and political anger. Both demonstrate how cynicism operates and show that if a leader is prepared to sacrifice all norms, he can – literally – get away with murder. Indeed, both plays dramatize the way a dictator is enabled by manipulating lesser men's ambitions and resorts to dreadful violence to shore up his power. It's a dynamic which Shakespeare would develop to dizzy-making effect in *Macbeth*.

Reading *Richard III* alongside *Arturo Ui* reminds us of the profoundly political nature of the Shakespeare's play and suggests the enduring relevance of Brecht's epilogue:

> Therefore learn how to see and not to gape.
> To act instead of talking all day long.
> The world was almost won by such an ape!
> The nations put him where his kind belong.
> But don't rejoice too soon at your escape –
> The womb he crawled from still is going strong.
>
> (CP, 1981, 99)

Can we imagine a production of *Richard III* which left the audience with a similar warning, especially in the light of the emergence of new strong men, new authoritarians?

Richard III and History

Richard III is a distinctly Elizabethan play, where the main characteristics of Shakespeare's youthful style are vividly on display: an epic structure bringing powerful forces into conflict with each other, a broad and dynamic social range, and a productive mixture of poetic and theatrical registers, all driven by a compelling but precisely plotted narrative. It's bold, confident and extraordinarily involving stuff.

A Brechtian production would show that the central action is merely the latest (if most lethal) development in a long-running struggle for power among the ruling elite, and one of the challenges is clarifying this political 'backstory': in other words, Richard's declaration that 'all the clouds that loured upon our house / [are] in the deep bosom of the ocean buried' (1.1.4) describes what is merely a temporary truce. England is already in deep trouble, and Richard's dictatorship plunges it into even greater darkness. Shakespeare relies on shared historical knowledge to achieve his ends, something that is vanishingly rare today. The Brechtian director will want to clarify it.

Richard, of course, also represents something new and there is a dynamic energy about him, a vividness which steps out of the medieval frame and connects with the popular Elizabethan audience in a way which is still mesmerising and alarming. The Brechtian director recognizes that populists, even the most reactionary ones, are also radicals and that Richard's rubbishing of traditional values grants him a charismatic appeal which other figures lack. And so the director would allow for the magnetism of such 'star appeal', even as they warn of its dangers.

The Brechtian director would also want to show that Richard rises at the expense of other people. They would chart the murders (before the action begins) of the young Prince Edward and his father, King Henry VI; Richard's seduction of Anne, Prince Edward's widow; the murder of his brother, the Duke of Clarence, as well as Hastings, the Lord Chamberlain; the murder of the junior royals, Rivers, Grey and Vaughan, as well as the killing of the two princes in the Tower; the poisoning of his wife, Anne; and, finally, the murder of his erstwhile ally and enabler, the Duke of Buckingham. If we are to understand that Richard's rise is more than merely 'evil', it needs to be shown as a political process, with each new death providing a further step in Richard's consolidation of power.

Such a production would also want to show the gathering opposition. At its heart is a trio of powerfully articulate women: Henry VI's widow, the implacable Queen Margaret; Lady Anne, whom Richard marries and then murders; and Elizabeth, widow of King Edward, whose daughter Richard decides he wants as his wife. Shakespeare shows each one realistically, each with their own vulnerabilities and passions, but together they articulate an alternative female perspective, and show that Richard's rise is, indeed, 'resistible'. Staging the opposition with conviction, strength and moral seriousness is essential.

Ultimately, of course, a military invasion from overseas is needed to bring down Richard's tyranny, and the Brechtian director would want to show Richmond's very different political and moral character. Brecht never directed a production of *Richard III* but one can only imagine the impact of the play on a German audience recently liberated from Hitler's dreadful tyranny.

'A Theatre Full of A-Effects!'

It's clear that *Richard III* would benefit from being staged with alienation.

'What misleads', Margot Heinemann explains, 'is not the degree of sympathy so much as the excessive concentration of interest and causation on the central character's mind and motives alone, and the magnetisation of the audience so that its own powers of judgement are paralysed' (1985, 239). 'If I want to see Richard III, I don't want to feel like Richard III', Brecht wrote. Instead, the 'phenomenon' of the central character should be observed in all its 'strangeness and incomprehensibility' (*BoT,* 1964, 27).

This can be helped by an understanding of the popular tradition from which it emerged. As Manfred Wekwerth explains, Richard was an extension of the popular figure of the 'Vice', whose monologues were intended as direct address:

> This entailed a doubling effect: the actor left his character for a few moments, came to the front of the stage and fraternized with the audience. In these passages... the text changes from one line to the next between the English of the courts and the English of the streets. Using this proletarian language, Richard – acting now as the Vice – seeks to win the audience's favour to accompany him in his daring attempt to get the crown, that only God can bestow, all by himself.
>
> (Wekwerth, 2012, 30)

This certainly catches something of the contradictory, improvised and elusive nature of Richard's performance in the popular theatre: attractive, charismatic and powerfully theatrical.

Understandably, modern directors often try to engage with the question of Richard's physical disabilities (the casting in 2024 of a non-disabled actor at Shakespeare's Globe caused an uproar). This is certainly one of the areas where the playwright's values contrast with modern sensitivities. Are we to understand Richard's disability as a metaphor for his malevolence, or should we, instead, see him as a realistic representation of the impact of society's negative attitudes towards people like him? This may require textual intervention to be credible and might limit the part's theatrical bravura, but is surely intriguing and perhaps necessary. It's certainly hard to know how we can achieve both, but the question shouldn't be ignored.

The Brechtian director should also explore the 'relative' quality of Richard's character and help the actor show that such charisma is not immutable. Rather, it changes according to circumstances and is consciously manipulated for political ends:

> THE ACTOR: And the fascination of Richard III: how can I illustrate that except by completely filling the character with it?
>
> THE DRAMATURG: You mean in the scene where he so fascinates the widow of the man he's murdered that she ends up falling for him? I can see two solutions. You either show that she's doing it out of sheer terror, or else you make her ugly. But however you show this fascination, it won't do you any good unless you can show how it fails him later in the play. So you need to show the relative power of fascination.
>
> (*BoP*, 2014, 104)

Thus, the actor would make clear what we know from our own world: that political leaders may enjoy enormous popular support one month and lose everything the next, and that it is incumbent on the rest of us to formulate a coherent opposition, whether by ridicule, facts or political action. The dictator's power may be considerable, but it has been artificially constructed and can be artificially deconstructed. Certainly, Shakespeare's King Richard on the eve of Bosworth Field, plagued by nightmares and desperate anxiety, has come a long way from the self-conscious and theatrical villain of the opening monologue.

Brecht's Dramaturg refers to this final scene as evidence for his claim that Shakespeare's theatre was 'full of A-effects!':

> There were no backcloths, so the writer took on the job of portraying the landscape. The stage didn't depict a specific area, it could be an entire heath. In *Richard III* (V.3), between the tents of Richard's and Richmond's camps, a ghost appears in both men's dreams, visible and audible to both of them and addressing itself to both.
>
> (*BoP*, 2014, 58)

Indeed, here Shakespeare's Brechtian technique is at its most pronounced, as the ghosts of the tyrant's many victims take it in turns to observe his downfall – reminding us forcefully that even the worst dictators will one day be defeated.

In the desire to avoid a simplistic happy ending, modern directors sometimes underplay this growing chorus. But they are the true political climax of the play: Richard may be prepared to give up his 'kingdom for a horse' but the people of his kingdom – whether murdered or, somehow, still clinging on – are determined to be rid of him once and for all. Indeed, they are the agents of his downfall, without whom the play lacks a dialectic, the very stuff of political drama.

The View from the Bottom

There is, of course, more to *Richard III* than a murderous struggle within the ruling elite, and a Brechtian production would track the impact of Richard's actions on the common people.

A good example is the pair of 'hardy, stout, resolved mates' (1.3.339) whom the ambitious Richard engages to murder his brother, the Duke of Clarence. When we first meet them, Richard is worried, recognizing that Clarence's rhetorical skills may 'move [their] hearts to pity' (348). The two soon gain access to their intended victim but, finding him asleep, the fear of God holds them back:

> SECOND MURDERER The urging of that word 'Judgement' hath bred a kind of remorse in me.
> FIRST MURDERER What? Art thou afraid?
> SECOND MURDERER Not to kill him, having a warrant, but to be damned for killing him, from the which no warrant can defend me.
> FIRST MURDERER I thought thou hadst been resolute.
> SECOND MURDERER So I am, to let him live.
>
> (1.4.107–14)

Importantly, Shakespeare has written something more than a mere pairing of opposites, for, in the best Brechtian fashion, these men are both bold *and* scared, eager *and* hesitant, and the Brechtian would insist on making these contradictions plain. What's more they are, of course, products of their time, and in them can be observed the tensions between the religious and the secular, the medieval and the early modern. Here, then, are Brecht's 'useful junction points'.

There's some irony in the Second Murderer's struggle to master his conscience, which he describes as a 'dangerous thing' that must be defeated. But Richard's promised 'reward' proves the best incentive:

> FIRST MURDERER Where's thy conscience now?
> SECOND MURDERER O, in the Duke of Gloucester's purse.
> FIRST MURDERER When he opens his purse to give us our reward, thy conscience flies out.
> SECOND MURDERER 'Tis no matter; let it go. There's few or none will entertain it.
> FIRST MURDERER What if it come to thee again?
> SECOND MURDERER I'll not meddle with it.
>
> (1.4.126–33)

Money, Brecht knows, is power. But the 'conscience' starts to affect the First Murderer too, though he thinks he can beat it in an open fight. It's a vivid dramatization – a Brechtian demystification, indeed – of the workings of the mind.

When Clarence wakes up, the first man is about to strike him, but his mate prefers to 'reason with him' (159). Both 'scarcely have the hearts to tell' (174) Clarence of their intentions, but his appeal makes no headway, and his confidence that his brother will protect him is greeted sceptically. Clarence makes some progress, imploring the two to 'relent, and save your souls' (255) but the First Murderer is unimpressed and kills 'the begging Prince' (266) from behind. Left alone, the Second compares himself to Pontius Pilate (271) and, giving up his fee, repents that 'the Duke is slain' (277). Meanwhile, his unrepentant colleague confesses that as soon as he's been paid, he'll go into hiding (281–2). Contradictory motivations and values have rarely been so brilliantly dramatized.

Peter Gill, the legendary director of working-class life, shrewdly noted that there's 'more to these characters than generalized portraits of low-life villainy about to meet princely sensitivity' (Gill, 2008, 78). Indeed, this episode is a good example of Brechtian realism – a chunk of that unvarnished 'raw material' that requires careful rehearsal and finely observed acting to bring to life. Done well, however, it can suggest the limits of the dictator's powers and the radical possibility that his orders might be disobeyed.

Another glimpse of life outside the aristocratic circle is Stanley's plea to the dying Edward IV for the life of his 'servant', 'who slew today a riotous gentleman' (2.1.100–1). The King contrasts his own natural inclination for mercy with the ruthlessness of his younger brother, but the episode reminds us of the precarious lives of the working people and the poor manners of many of their masters.

A further sighting are the worried citizens in 2.3. At one point the Third Citizen offers a perfect *exempla* of Brecht's gestic poetry:

When clouds are seen, wise men put on their cloaks;
When great leaves fall, then winter is at hand;
When the sun sets, who doth not look for night?
Untimely storms make men expect a dearth.
All may be will; but if God sort it so,
'Tis more than we deserve, or I expect.

(2.3.32–7)

He could be a Berlin Jew confronted by his damaged shop the morning after *Kristallnacht*.

Or look at the anonymous Scrivener who appears with an official document in his hand and explains that he has spent eleven hours writing out the 'indictment of the good lord Hastings':

> Which in a set hand fairly is engrossed,
> That it may be today read o'er in Paul's.
> And mark how well the sequel hangs together:
> Eleven hours I spent to write it over,
> For yesternight by Catesby was it sent me;
> The precedent was full as long a-doing;
> And yet within these five hours Lord Hastings lived,
> Untainted, unexamined, free, at liberty.
> Here's a good world the while. Who is so gross
> That cannot see this palpable device?
> Yet who so blind but says he sees it not?
> Bad is the world, and all will come to nought
> When such ill dealings must be seen in thought.
>
> (3.6.1–14)

The Scrivener knows that Hastings has already been killed and that this 'palpable device' merely supplies bureaucratic cover to arbitrary rule. The perspective of this lowly figure (a member of what one historian wonderfully dubbed the 'proletariat of inky toilers', Hale, 1993, 79) helps us understand the actions of the mighty: they are 'alienated' in such a way that we can see them for what they are. Tyranny, as Hitler's regime showed, requires bureaucrats to help, and this speech, with its complicity with the popular audience, recruits our support for the resistance. It is a case study in Brechtian alienation.

Richard's wish to be rid of the two princes in the Tower requires someone to do the deed, and Shakespeare draws James Tyrrel with scrupulous care. In 4.2 we see his readiness to carry out Richard's whispered instructions, but the moment this has happened, he expresses regret:

> The tyrannous and bloody act is done,
> The most arch deed of piteous massacre

That ever yet this land was guilty of.
Dighton and Forrest, who I did suborn
To do this piece of ruthful butchery,
Albeit they were fleshed villains, bloody dogs,
Melted with tenderness and mild compassion,
Wept like to children in their deaths' sad story.

(4.3.1–8)

When quizzed, his despair is palpable, but not enough to stop him from visiting the King 'soon at after-supper' to discuss his reward. Murdering children is a challenging business, and 'the great realist' presents it in all its contradiction.

Shakespeare draws the messengers who bring Richard news of the gathering of the armed opposition with care, even showing the man who brings favourable news being abused by the King who presumes it must be bad (4.4.509–14). And then in two parallel addresses to their (seemingly silent) troops, first by Richmond (5.3.237–70) and then by Richard (314–41), we see contrasting attitudes to the men they are leading. From these counterpointed public speeches, the popular audience draws its own conclusions about which leader they would want to follow. Here, as elsewhere, *Richard III* offers a case study in Brecht's theatrical technique.

Provocations, Exercises and Practical Suggestions

- Richard has a physical disability. If your group has a disabled person, ask him/her to read the opening speech. If no one has a physical disability, experiment with different ways of expressing such disability (a wheelchair, crutches etc.). Does a genuinely disabled actor help the audience understand Richard? Is the story relevant to the modern debate about disability rights and, if so, how? Is there any value in 'cripping up', allowing the performance of physical disability be a way of 'alienating' the audience and seeing Richard as a 'grotesque' and 'unnatural' murderer. How can these complicated issues be resolved?

- Divide your group into two and cast one actor from each in the roles of Ui and Richard. Ask each half to create a five-minute presentation of the action as told from the perspective of the title role: 'He decided to do this, he decided to do that.' See where the two plays are similar but also where they differ. And explore the different ways that the central character's relationship with the audience can be both appealing and appalling.
- Rehearse the scene of Clarence's murder (1.4) and see how many points of sympathy you can establish for the two murderers. Tell the two actors to draw attention to their poverty, reluctance and kindness. Ask them to improvise short monologues which explain the realities of their lives: perhaps one of them is looking after a sick mother, the other can't get decent work because of the colour of his skin and so on. Ask them to explain the role of religion in their lives and their fear of divine retribution. Search the scene for biblical resonances and explore their political, social and psychological implications. Above all, show that they're simply doing a job and that it is Richard who is to blame.
- Explore all this in a comic fashion: put a slice of chocolate cake on the table and tell the actors that if they eat it they will be punished. Then remind them that they haven't eaten anything for three days (and no chocolate for two months). Establish what they have to gain from carrying out their commission, but also what they might lose.
- Stage the scene (5.3) on the evening before the battle and see how Shakespeare uses counterpointed voices and figures to create his effects. Work out how to arrange it in such a way that everyone who appears on stage (whether a ghost or a living person) can be seen by the audience. Explore what would be lost if that wasn't achieved. And discuss why Brecht hails the scene as being 'full of A-effects'.
- Consider the points of similarity between Richard's story and the career of a modern populist politician. Think about the points of similarity but also the differences. Look through the play and give each scene a 'legend': 'In the same

way that Vladimir Putin found himself increasingly isolated after the invasion of Ukraine, so Richard III on the eve of Bosworth Field is all alone in his tent.' But also differences: 'Whereas Donald Trump would like to kill off his political rivals, Richard III is able to get away with it' or 'Like Boris Johnson, Richard III expects utter loyalty from his supporters and is astonished when they abandon him.'

As You Like It

A Tale of Two Courts

There are only a handful of mentions of *As You Like It* in Brecht's writing. Perhaps the most intriguing is his account of Charles Laughton reading scenes aloud to him in Santa Monica. This is a shame because the play's tale of exile from a dictatorship and the many contradictions that it throws up should surely have struck a chord. It's possible, however, that its predominantly rural setting held little interest for the great dramatist of modern life, and that its emphasis on romantic love struck him as irrelevant: after all, Brecht had agreed with the Marxist sociologist Fritz Sternberg that the First World War 'had ended the comparatively short period which had begun with *Romeo and Juliet*, the period in which sexual love could be central to a work of art' (Hayman, 1983, 122). And so, in exploring a Brechtian approach to the play, I will be more than usually dependent on hypothesis.

Perhaps because of the scenic allure of the Forest of Arden, directors and designers sometimes overlook the crucial early scenes at the court. But it's here that we see the emergence of a new, dictatorial style of government, providing the essential frame for what follows. There is no clear explanation for Duke Frederick's banishment of his elder brother (other than ambition and greed), nor the young nobleman Oliver's persecution of his brother, Orlando. What is clear, however, is that both are representative of the acquisitive individualism that was transforming Shakespeare's England where, increasingly, Cain triumphed over Abel and inherited the earth. This may be an ancient tale, but a production that did not see it as representing a fundamental shift in political and moral values (one of Brecht's 'useful junction points') will fail to catch the play's underlying tensions.

The biblically named retainer Adam has sometimes been mocked for his selflessness, but a Brechtian director would approach him with more circumspection: yes, the ancient servant who sacrifices everything for his master can seem a conservative stooge, but Adam's long life (he was born before the Dissolution of the Monasteries, like an old man today born before the Second World War) should command more respect. The Brechtian director would focus on Adam's decision to hand over his impressive savings (2.3.38–55) and understand the contradictions involved: as a generous gesture in contrast to the behaviour of his betters but, simultaneously, a financial sacrifice against his best interests. After all, Adam doesn't have to go into exile with Orlando, and a good production would find ways of highlighting that choice and the circumstances under which it is made.

To bring this out, the Brechtian director might ask the actor playing Le Beau to refer to the audience when he hopes for 'a better world than this' (1.2.273), and encourage the actor playing Orlando to actively challenge our own values in his praise for Adam:

O good old man, how well in thee appears
The constant service of the antique world,
Where servants sweat for duty not for meed.
Thou art not for the fashion of these times,
Where none will sweat but for promotion,
And having that do choke their service up
Even with the having.

(2.3.56–62)

Such complicity does not necessarily endorse the speaker's views, but it does make us question our own times and consider the very different values of the past. Playing with 'alienation' makes such contradictions evident and helps us understand Adam's motivation.

The relationship between master and man takes on the dimensions of a biblical parable when the two men (reminiscent, perhaps, of the maidservant and the baby in *The Caucasian Chalk Circle*) flee into exile. The young aristocrat goes off in search of food to sustain the frail old manservant and carries him in his arms to safety. In his challenge to the gathered exiles, Orlando generalizes his and Adam's individual story into a broader pleading:

> If ever you have looked on better days,
> If ever been where bells have knolled to church,
> If ever sat at any good man's feast,
> If ever from your eyelids wiped a tear,
> And know what 'tis to pity and be pitied –
>
> (2.7.114–9)

And, finally, he makes us consider society's duties to the elderly:

> There is an old poor man
> Who after me hath many a weary step
> Limped in pure love. Till he be first sufficed,
> Oppressed with two weak evils, age and hunger,
> I will not touch a bit.
>
> (2.7.130–4)

In a Brechtian production, Orlando's 'two weak evils' might remind us of the founder of the welfare state, William Beveridge, and his five 'giant evils': want, disease, ignorance, squalor and idleness. Certainly, by taking this episode seriously, the Brechtian director will show that it is only when the young man remembers his duties to the vulnerable that he deserves Rosalind's love. If this parable lacks the ironic content so often found in Brecht, the construction of a moral fable from simple narrative units is reminiscent of *The Caucasian Chalk Circle* and *Mother Courage*, plays whose debt to Shakespeare is evident.

Carefully tracking the journey of these men into exile (along with Celia, Rosalind and Touchstone) will help us understand the Forest of Arden not just as a location for psychological cure but political refuge: Duke Senior has escaped his brother's persecution but also his dictatorial style of government. And so, the audience will be encouraged to ask where the real court lies: in the hierarchical violence of Duke Frederick's dictatorship or 'under the greenwood tree' where peace and good company can, it seems, be found? By showing these as representing diametrically opposing ways of thinking, the dialectic will become vivid.

The Brechtian director would want to clarify that this may be a conflict within the ruling elite, but it has consequences for all. What they shouldn't do is ignore the stubborn fact of exile: indeed, a Brechtian production would show that the first half of the play deals with the fact of migration above all else. This doesn't (necessarily) require the imagery of people in small boats crossing the Channel: what it does need is to take the story seriously and engage with the multiple transformations that it enacts. As ever, tracking change is essential.

The 'Uncouth Forest'

The Forest of Arden, to which these refugees flee, is an intriguing mixture of the pastoral and the realistic, the ordinary and the fantastical, but in Shakespeare's portraits of those who live there we find an image of everyday existence. Karl Marx and Friedrich Engels spoke contemptuously of 'the idiocy of rural life' but Brecht, John Willett reminds us, saw 'the peasants as quite as important as (and, if anything, more interesting than) the industrial proletariat' (Willett, 1984, 206).

Shakespeare is similarly respectful. Indeed, in his portrait of the old shepherd Corin, he draws a figure of exceptional dignity, even featuring a perfect embodiment of Marx's theory of the alienation of labour:

> I am shepherd to another man
> And do not shear the fleeces that I graze.
>
> (2.4.77–8)

Then, in his confrontation with the defiantly urban Touchstone, we hear the voice of a forgotten group, the rural poor:

> Sir, I am a true labourer. I earn that I eat, get that I wear; owe no man hate, envy no man's happiness; glad of other men's good, content with my harm; and the greatest of my pride is to see my ewes graze and my lambs suck.
>
> (3.2.70–4)

The Brechtian director would do whatever they could to give these class-based observations the space that they deserve.

The director might also suggest something of the changing nature of the Elizabethan countryside and recognize that while the forest offered refuge from the centralizing state, it was gradually being encroached on; they might even try to suggest the process of deforestation that posed such a threat to people living on the land, whose dependence on 'chalk' (free grazing sheep) was being directly challenged by the growth of 'cheese' (dairy cows in enclosed fields). The danger, of course, lies in irrelevant sociological detail, but the fact that Phoebe and Silvius are described as 'shepherds' should alert us to the fact that an Elizabethan 'forest' is a large area of common (or royal) land, and not necessarily the dense woodland of many a stage design.

The director should also take seriously the challenges of a life lived largely out of doors (the aristocratic Celia buys a cottage) and note how many references there are to 'winter and rough weather' (2.5.7 and 39), 'uncouth forest' (2.6.7) and 'bleak air' (15), as well as the 'winter wind' (2.1.7 and 2.7.175) and the 'bitter sky' (185). The countryside might offer refuge from the corruption and persecution of the city, and its natural beauties provide its own consolation, especially in the spring and summer, but it has its own challenges, which are best faced down by cooperation and community. It's not all bucolic paradise.

A detail, perhaps, but the director would be wise to attend to the position of 3.1, which returns the action to the court after the allure of the country. This scene is often repositioned (or sometimes cut) to allow for a fuller scenic transition to the forest (and, sometimes, the doubling of the two dukes), but Shakespeare's epic structure asks us to hold both courts in a dialectical relationship. Duke Frederick's orders to Oliver are particularly brutal:

> Find out thy brother wheresoe'er he is;
> Seek him with candle. Bring him dead or living
> Within this twelvemonth, or turn thou no more
> To seek a living in our territory.
>
> (3.1.5–8)

And with this, Oliver's status is suddenly reversed and he, too, is sent into exile:

> Thy lands, and all things that thou dost call thine
> Worth seizure, do we seize unto our hands,

> Till thou canst quit thee by thy brother's mouth
> Of what we think against thee.
>
> (3.1.9–12)

In this brave new world, no one is spared, and in Frederick's peremptory and careless orders ('Well, push him out of doors', 3.1.15), we can hear the still greater brutality of *King Lear*.

Back in Arden, the melancholic Jacques rewards some scrutiny. We're told that he was once 'a libertine' who bears 'all th'embossed sores and headed evils' (2.7.67) of venereal disease and, in what is (ultimately) a romantic comedy, represents a very different way of being: indeed, Charles Laughton, himself gay, told Brecht that he wanted to see Jacques 'played as [a] homosexual' – along with Osric from *Hamlet* and the 'clown bringing a basket' in *Antony and Cleopatra* (J, 1993, 325–6). We're told that 'most invectively [he] pierceth through / The body of country, city, court' (2.1.58) and describes Senior's court as 'mere usurpers, tyrants and what's worse, / To fright the animals and to kill them up' (161–2). At one point, he even declares his wish to be a licensed fool:

> Give me leave
> To speak my mind, and I will through and through
> Cleanse the foul body of th'infected world
> If they will patiently receive my medicine.
>
> (2.7.58–61)

Jacques' desire to become an independent-minded satirist, lacking in status but granted license to say what he thinks, should be attended to; after all, new perspectives, fresh ways of thinking, from his expression of animal rights to the apparent wisdom of such marginalized figures, play an essential role in any dialectical progress.

At the same time, however, Jacques' philosophy is largely cerebral and sorely tested when held up against lived experience. His famous speech 'All the world's a stage' (2.7.140–67) reduces life to a series of performances, which have little value beyond themselves. In many ways it's a counsel of despair whose final cadence ('*Sans* teeth, *sans* eyes, *sans* taste, *sans* everything') is borne out by the arrival of old Adam carried in Orlando's arms, but then immediately contradicted by the primal act of charity that follows (reviving Adam). Thus, in the Brechtian theatre, Jacques is subjected to 'alienation', and we are encouraged to ask what wisdom this upper-class misanthrope really offers.

'Country Copulatives'

As the play's romantic elements coalesce, the Brechtian director would show that the four pairs of lovers are defined by their class as much as their personalities, and are best understood in contradistinction to each other.

Thus, the sudden love match of Celia and the reformed Oliver, with its lofty talk of a 'bloody napkin' and dangerous animals, along with the political harmony promised by such a pairing, is distinctly aristocratic in tone. By contrast, the relationship between Oliver's younger brother Orlando and Rosalind, the daughter of the exiled Duke Senior, is more informal, conducted almost entirely in prose and shaped by the power reversal created by Rosalind's disguise as a boy. And this, the Brechtian director will show, may have less political capital, but more personal investment. Above all, by giving Rosalind the power and allowing both figures to feel the full humiliation of erotic obsession, their story champions the emerging idea of the companionate marriage, and feels strikingly modern as a result: 'Men have died from time to time and worms have eaten them, but not for love' (4.1.97–9), observes Rosalind drily, and one of the most intriguing aspects of their relationship is how the complex nature of romantic love is made plain through disguise, playacting and distinctly anti-romantic jokes.

The asymmetrical relationship between the two shepherds, the love-struck Silvius and the contemptuous Phoebe, is drawn from pastoral, and what's striking is the lofty tone of their language (entirely in verse), but also the surprising fact that Silvius seems to have some money. Thus, although they are hardly gentry, Shakespeare goes out of his way to lift them above the forest poor, and the Brechtian director should attend to such details. But this doesn't protect them from the condescension of Rosalind, who decides to educate both in the way of love, calling Silvius a 'tame snake' and confronting Phoebe contemptuously:

>   Who might be your mother,
> That you insult, exult, and all at once
> Over the wretched? What though you have no beauty –
> As by my faith I see no more in you
> Than without candle may go to bed –
> Must you be therefore proud and pitiless?
>
>   (3.5.36–41)

And when Phoebe falls for the disguised 'Ganymede', Rosalind is brutal:

> But, mistress, know yourself: down on your knees,
> And thank heaven fasting for a good man's love.
> For I must tell you friendly in your ear:
> Sell when you can, you are not for all markets.
>
> (3.5.58–61)

Upwardly mobile peasants don't stand a chance when confronted by the flower of the English aristocracy, it seems, and the Brechtian director would do well to let this uncomfortable confrontation be more than mere comedy. Rosalind is certainly no political radical.

The lowest class couple are the goatherd Audrey and the fool Touchstone, who manages to steal her from her true love, the 25-year-old forest dweller William. It's a relationship in which both stand to gain but is hardly characterized by 'true love', and Audrey's prospects as Touchstone's wife are uncomfortable. The overarching philosophical, political point is that at the end all eight are subject to the (somewhat mechanistic) blessings of Hymen (5.4.106–44) and the play suggests that in matters of sex and reproduction, class differences seemingly melt away. It's a curious kind of 'levelling up', one dependent on the heterosexual promise of new life, but *As You Like It*'s 'wide and universal theatre' (2.7.138) deconstructs class and society and allows tentative glimpses of the 'better world' (1.2.273) that Brecht so urgently sought.

Provocations, Exercises and Practical Suggestions

- Consider three alternative outcomes in the opening movement of the play:
    - Orlando is killed by Charles the Wrestler.
    - Rosalind doesn't fall for Orlando.
    - Adam doesn't leave for the forest with Orlando.

    Locate the critical moments when these alternatives might manifest themselves and ask your group to improvise alternative story lines. Then return to the text and work out what you can do to make an audience think that these are possible. Thus, in staging the wrestling match, ask your fight director to find a moment when everyone thinks that Orlando is about to be knocked out; consider a moment when Rosalind doesn't notice Orlando until he wins (maybe she has been cheering on Charles, or perhaps is just uninterested in wrestling); and experiment with Adam worried about handing over his money (maybe he gives his purse to Orlando, snatches it back and then gives it again). All of these will show that the fundamentally positive outcomes in the play are the consequence of particular decisions and could have been different.

- Adam declares that he has saved 500 crowns. Research how much that would be worth today and explore how much he must have put aside every month. If the play is set in 1599 (when it was first staged), Adam (who says he is 'now almost four score') would have been born in 1519, under Henry VIII and before the 'Break from Rome'. What does this suggest about his values and world view?

- Ask your group to read 2.4 and see what it says about the real-life conditions of the Elizabethan countryside. Write a monologue for Corin which describes his working day: use as much of Shakespeare's text as you can, but add your own inventions.

- Read the scene (5.1) with Audrey and William, and explore the extent to which they are exploited by the city dwellers. Suggest to the actor playing Touchstone that he plays him as a working-class Londoner (a Cockney even), in despair at the simplicity of two forest dwellers who've never left their village. But also see what it would take to show that both Audrey and William have minds of their own and offer an alternative viewpoint. Highlight the points where Shakespeare grants them dignity and try to rescue them from the 'enormous condescension of posterity'.

- Examine the four romantic relationships in the play and try to identify what brings the eight lovers together in class terms. Explore the extent to which the match between Oliver and Celia is a political, aristocratic one; Rosalind and Orlando an individualistic, companionate marriage;

Sylvius and Phoebe the lovesick shepherd and shepherdess of classical pastoral, and Audrey and Touchstone a highly sexualized and mutually exploitative coupling. Ask each actor to highlight in green his or her romantic statements, and in red any anti-romantic ones. Play these in contradiction with each other.
- Identify the shifting forms in the play, from lofty classical verse to earthy prose, pastoral one moment, naturalism the next and see how Hymen represents yet another genre. Examine how these shifting forms express shifting belief systems.
- Explore Jacques' misanthropy and see how his attitudes offer critical ballast to the play's romantic lovers, but also consider to what extent a modern audience is likely to reject him. Work through the play from Jacques' point of view and see the extent of his aristocratic contempt for his fellow humans.
- 'Sluttishness may come hereafter', jokes Touchstone cruelly about Audrey. Devise a one-minute drama which shows what happens to all the characters after Shakespeare's play is over. Who is happily married, who unhappily?
- And now imagine the opposite: thus, it's often assumed that Touchstone and Audrey will be unhappy but that Rosalind and Orlando will experience true love. What might the opposite look like?
- Devise a production of *As You Like It* which dispenses with all scenery: offer a simple white box with clear bright light, no furniture and only hand props. What is gained; what is lost?

Measure for Measure

An 'Unperformable' Adaptation

Brecht was evidently fascinated by *Measure for Measure*, which he hailed as 'the most philosophical of Shakespeare's works, certainly his most progressive'. The play, he explained, 'demands from those in positions of authority that they shouldn't measure others by standards different from those by which they themselves would be judged [and] ought not demand of their subjects a moral stance which they cannot adopt themselves' (*CP*, 2001, viii–ix). It's not a wildly original reading of Shakespeare's great 'problem play', but it does, at least, engage with its social and political content.

These comments appeared in a theatre journal accompanying the Copenhagen premiere of Brecht's *Round Heads and Pointed Heads*. Originally a commercial proposition – 'To think that this too was conceived as a gold mine!', he complained (*L*, 1990, 130) – Brecht's complex but frankly counterproductive methods resulted, after twelve long drafts, in an entirely new text in which Shakespeare's original play is almost completely obscured.

Surprisingly, perhaps, Brecht used *Measure for Measure* as a springboard for an ambitious exploration of the topical – if toxic – question of racism and its complex connection with class politics, all set in an imaginary South American country. Hailed by the constructivist playwright Sergei Tretyakov as a 'direct satire' on National Socialism and praised by the exiled Austrian screenwriter and theatre director Berthold Viertel as 'the only political comedy of the Germans which contains considerable thoughts' (Witt, 1975, 79, 82–3), Brecht's play – which he himself described as 'unperformable' (*L*, 1990, 130) – is unloved and hardly ever revived.

Following its premiere in 1936, Brecht defended *Round Heads and Pointed Heads* against two objections. The first was that 'the play brings grist to the fascist mill with the fascist assertion that Aryans have visibly (and anatomically) different racial characteristics from Jews':

> Obviously, it is no more fascist to take note of racial differences than to contend, as some Jews do, that no such differences exist. It would not do the oppressed Negroes in the United States much good if someone were to demand equal rights on the ground that they are white.

The second objection was that Brecht 'was not giving a picture of fascism, because fascism cannot happen in an agrarian country'. Brecht's reply was that 'This is true as far as it goes', but explained:

> Since my purpose was to depict racism, I was able to get by with my camouflage (an agrarian setting). Racism is used to deceive the people, not only by German fascism (which in this, incidentally, differs from Italian fascism) but also by other revolutionary governments, and has been since time immemorial.
> (*L*, 1990, 245)

The obscurity of all this – with the distinct possibility that Brecht was underestimating the Nazis' genocidal intentions – is typical of the entire undertaking. But, as Brecht's English editors insist, 'the use of racist politics, or even war, as a calculated distraction from social and economic problems is depressingly familiar'. Indeed, although the play 'may in retrospect seem inadequate to Nazism, [it] has a great deal of relevance to later twentieth century conflicts on several continents' (*CP*, 2001, xi).

Margot Heinemann, meanwhile, offers a useful feminist perspective. Writing about how Brecht's Isabella employs a sex worker to stand in for her promised assignment with Angelo, she reminds us that in Shakespeare, 'Mariana too is vulnerable because she's poor, her dowry having been lost at sea'. She adds that 'Brecht's main dramatic point, that the gentry can usually find someone else to suffer the unpleasant experiences for them, is hinted at again in *Measure* in comic form, when the Duke hunts around for a low-class convict to be executed so that his head can be sent to satisfy

Angelo.' It's a characteristically astute way of allowing Brecht to cast light on the original: 'Beneath the surface of Shakespeare's reassuringly happy ending lurks a very nasty underworld of sexual and commercial exploitation of inferiors, which is never cleaned up, only played down and obscured.' In Brecht's adaptation, she explains, 'this side of the contradiction becomes the central impression' (Heinemann, 1994, 244).

Brecht retained his interest in the play and describes how listening to Charles Laughton read it aloud gave him insights into a living tradition:

> Although L's theatrical experience had been in a London which had become thoroughly indifferent to the theatre, the old Elizabethan London still lived in him, the London where theatre was such a passion that it could swallow important works of art greedily and barefacedly simply as 'texts'.
>
> (*BoP*, 2014, 155)

We can only guess what the mature Brecht would have done had he attempted a fresh adaptation of *Measure for Measure* for the Berliner Ensemble.

Measure for Measure and the Sex Industry

At the heart of Shakespeare's play is the catastrophic impact of the poor decisions of the mighty on their subjects. Thus, the Duke's decision to hand over power to his puritanical deputy might have its own spiritual, educational and personal motivations, but it also exposes his subjects to a regime which has no understanding of human realities and leads to even greater distress. In his portrait of Angelo, Shakespeare lays bare the hypocrisy of puritanical moralizing, with dire consequences not just on the sex industry but on young nobility such as Claudio, his pregnant girlfriend Juliet and his sister, the novice Isabella. The action shows up the structures of power, and the very notion of authority is alienated.

Modern productions sometimes condemn Angelo's actions as an assault on female bodily autonomy, while, simultaneously, celebrating the sex industry as a liberating alternative to oppressive puritanism: one kind of exploitation is good; the other is bad, it seems. The result, ironically, is like a lazy version of *The Threepenny Opera*, with scantily dressed young women dancing provocatively under red lightbulbs, while the audience is enraged by the powerful Angelo's abusive treatment of the well-bred Isabella. But, as both Brecht and Shakespeare understood, commercial sex is a degrading and exploitative way of earning a living, and the 'great realist' knew that the immediate consequence of Vienna's 'houses of resort' being 'plucked down' (1.2.93) was an economic hit on the people who work in them. Certainly the Brechtian director would want to engage closely with these questions.

Sadly, there is some textual confusion in the hundred or so lines in 1.2 when the sex industry is discussed, and the Brechtian director would want to make sense of this 'raw material', which includes magnificent shards of everyday realism, such as Mistress Overdone's great lament:

> Thus, what with the war, what with the sweat, what with the gallows, and what with poverty, I am custom-shrunk.
> (1.2.79–81)

This could be the voice of Mother Courage herself. It's just a shame that, beyond a passing reference to one Kate Keepdown, the play doesn't feature any of the young women who keep her in business.

In Overdone's pimp, however, the bombastically named Pompey, Shakespeare has created a working man of extraordinary invention, wit and self-confidence. Look at the way he bamboozles his judges and casts scurrilous aspersions on the constable's wife:

> Sir, she came in great with child, and longing, saving your honour's reverence, for stewed prunes; sir, we had but two in the house, which at that very distant time stood, as it were, in a fruit dish – a dish of some threepence – your honours have seen such dishes – they are not china dishes, but very good dishes.
> (2.1.85–90)

There's a lot more of this brilliant filibustering which drives his judges to distraction. When finally dismissed with the threat of a whipping, Pompey offers a mock-heroic soliloquy (addressed directly to the audience) which goes to the heart of his irrepressible energy:

> Whip me? No, no; let carman whip his jade.
> The valiant heart's not whipped out of his trade.
>
> (2.1.244–5)

Thus, Pompey is, as he declares, 'a poor fellow that would live' and while a Brechtian production would not sentimentalize him, it would not ignore the 'bottom-up' perspective that he offers so vividly.

Pompey is soon arrested and sent to prison. But there again, Shakespeare offers realistic insights, this time into the politics of incarceration: the kindly Provost knows that the justice that is being meted out has its flaws, but is diligent in obeying orders; meanwhile, the executioner Abhorson is a professional who doesn't want amateurs involved in his gruesome trade, the hardened prisoner Barnardine refuses to succumb to the simplistic demands of his betters, and Pompey muses drily that he is 'as well acquainted' in the prison as he was in his 'old house of profession'. All these figures play a crucial role in the play's dialectical structure, and the Brechtian director would insist that they are not simplified, patronized or cut.

#MeToo

The aristocratic story at the heart of *Measure for Measure* – Angelo's attempt to sleep with Isabella as a condition for her brother's life – exposes the corruptions of power. The tale of a powerful man professing moral superiority while preying on young women is an ancient one. But, as is often the case in Shakespeare, this became especially relevant a few years ago.

Furious at Angelo for his indecent proposal, Isabella threatens to denounce him in public:

> Sign me a present pardon for my brother,
> Or with an outstretched throat I'll tell the world aloud
> What man thou art.
>
> (2.4.151–3)

Angelo's reply is chillingly cynical ('Who will believe thee, Isabel?', 154) and, restating his demand with renewed confidence and dreadful sadism, walks off: 'As for you, / Say what you can, my false o'erweighs your true' (69–70). With this, Isabella, standing alone on the broad stage, turns to the audience and poses the very question that epitomized the entire #MeToo movement:

> To whom should I complain? Did I tell this
> Who would believe me?
>
> (2.4.171–2)

Thus, Isabella isn't simply the victim of a personal injustice, she lives in a society in which her word will not be believed. As Angelo puts it:

> My unsoiled name, th'austereness of my life,
> My vouch against you and my place i'th' state
> Will so your accusation overweigh
> That you shall stifle in your own report
> And smell of calumny.
>
> (2.4.155–9)

The Brechtian director would want to show that Isabella's powerlessness isn't merely personal, it is shared by generations of young women in the face of powerful men's predations.

As ever, however, and as Brecht taught us, we should be alert to the contradictions. For even as we expose the structures of male power, we should remember that Isabella falls back on a misguided and class-based belief in Claudio's nobility:

> I'll to my brother;
> Though he hath fallen by prompture of the blood,
> Yet hath he in him such a mind of honour
> That had he twenty heads to tender down
> On twenty bloody blocks, he'd yield them up
> Before his sister should her body stoop
> To such abhorred pollution.
>
> (2.4.177–83)

Her conclusion, addressed directly to the audience, and played with alienation, should shock us with its single-minded conclusion:

> Then Isabel live chaste, and brother die:
> More than our brother is our chastity.
>
> (2.4.184–5)

Indeed, Isabella soon discovers that the world doesn't fit into her neat schemes: her brother tries to be brave – as his class (and the memory of their dead parents) requires – but soon, in distinctly ignoble and tearful desperation, he begs her sister to give in to Angelo's demands. As a result, brother and sister (who I often imagine are twins) part from each other in shared humiliation and rage:

> Thy sin's not accidental, but a trade;
> Mercy to thee would prove itself a bawd.
> 'Tis best that thou diest quickly.
>
> (3.1.155–7)

As so often, the Brechtian insists, victims of oppression blame each other for their oppression, instead of turning their fire on the real enemy.

Observing this contradiction must not be misunderstood. I'm certainly not minimizing the grotesque treatment that Isabella faces. But Brecht would argue that such dialectical thinking helps us focus on the real substance: Claudio isn't 'wrong' to ask Isabella to sleep with Angelo, but nor is Isabella 'wrong' in refusing him; the problem is that justice depends on the law being executed in a way that is transparent, objective and fair; it also needs to allow for the complicated truths of life, the unvarnished 'raw material' which cannot be contained by mere moralism. And so here, as ever, the audience is being asked to look beyond the individual to the structures of power that shape, deliver and so often pervert the course of justice. We're familiar with the notion of 'institutional sexism': Shakespeare (as filtered through Brecht) is asking us to explore it in the system of justice.

Isabella and the Elusive Duke

The Duke of Vienna, who carries the overall responsibility for what goes wrong, is a notoriously elusive figure. One of the knotty questions the Brechtian director needs to answer is why he hands over his power to Angelo in the first place, and in such haste. Shakespeare gives little clue – other than the suggestion that this is a test of Free Will – but in his meeting with Friar Thomas (1.3) we learn that he has allowed bad behaviour to go unpunished:

> Lord Angelo is precise,
> Stands at a guard with envy, scarce confesses
> That his blood flows, or that his appetite
> Is more to bread than stone. Hence shall we see,
> If power change purpose, what our seemers be.
>
> (1.3.50–4)

Played with alienation, and a direct relationship with the audience, such a speech should prompt us to ask why this experiment is required. Indeed, the confusion about the Duke's motives might give us pause: if his reasons are so murky, the corruption in Vienna is coming from the top.

We next meet the Duke in the prison when, disguised as a friar, he is advising the condemned young Claudio on how to 'be absolute for death'. His is a strangely glib lesson (if steeped in theology) but it does at least establish that he is involved in an educational project (3.1.1–43). Overhearing Claudio's agonising meeting with Isabella (54–158), however, offers him a more vivid lesson in human suffering and soon, deploying disguise in a way that a Brechtian production will suggest is questionable, he sets out to solve the problem that his own actions have brought about. His methods, which include a dramatic shifting of genre from bitter realism to escapist romance, introduce a novel solution: substituting for Isabella the long suffering and poverty-stricken Mariana, still eager to consummate her marriage to Angelo. Such a dramatic shift of style allows for a shift in emphasis and the possibility of a different kind of resolution, and a Brechtian production would find ways (music, lighting, imagery) of suggesting the changes in genre.

Shakespeare's dialectical realism, however, soon allows for powerful criticism of the Duke's actions from the mouth of the licentious young gentleman Lucio (indeed, their long scene together – 3.1.352–442 – *can* be played with Lucio knowing exactly who the friar is). The Duke also encounters buoyant defiance from Pompey and Mistress Overdone. And, finally, when Angelo insists on the death of Claudio despite (supposedly) having slept with Isabella, the Duke's best plans come to naught, and he's forced to improvise. Hearing of one Barnardine, who is to be executed later, the Duke asks the Provost to send *his* head to Angelo instead of Claudio's. And, meeting with understandable resistance from the Provost ('Pardon me, good father, it is against my oath', 4.2.179), employs the beguiling cadences of the Annunciation to lull the Provost into submission:

> Look, th'unfolding star calls up the shepherd. Put not yourself into amazement how these things should be; all difficulties are but easy when they are known.
> (4.2.199–202)

The religious will claim that Shakespeare is deliberately presenting the Duke (disguised as a friar) as divinely inspired; the more sceptical will argue that resorting to such language is manipulative. By bringing out its biblical language, a careful production can suggest both.

With Barnardine's stubborn refusal, Shakespeare shows yet again how real life resists such moralizing and we, like the Duke himself, are confronted with the view from the ground (like the 'straw' in Barnardine's cell that Pompey hears 'rustle', perhaps? 4.3.33–4). The Duke's plan is rescued by an even more extravagant story, the death of a 'cruel fever' of 'One Ragozine, a most notorious pirate' (4.3.69), who resembles Claudio and whose decapitated head will trick Angelo into thinking that his order has been carried out. And these many shifts of register – too convenient, too tidy, too miraculous, perhaps? – have the effect of returning us to what really matters.

For it is at this moment that the Duke's methods become most questionable. He announces, in a speech which, done well, should provoke murmurs of critical protest from a lively audience, that:

> I will keep her ignorant of her good
> To make her heavenly comforts of despair
> When it is least expected.
>
> (4.3.107–9)

And soon he lies to her that her brother is dead: 'He hath released him, Isabel, from the world' (4.3.113). How much cruelty is Isabella meant to withstand? But, as ever, Shakespeare demands what Brecht called 'complex seeing': insisting that positive ends might require questionable means is a moral challenge that Brecht was all too familiar with. And the audience's attention should also be drawn to the *ad hominem* nature of Isabella's rage ('O, I will to him and pluck out his eyes', 4.3.117) and her expression of near existential despair:

> Unhappy Claudio, wretched Isabel
> Injurious world, most damned Angelo.
>
> (4.3.119–20)

The future for everybody seems utterly bleak.

Shakespeare isn't finished, however, and the action comes to its climax in the play's mighty Act Five, and nowhere more powerfully than the moment when Mariana urges Isabella to join her in petitioning the Duke for the life of the disgraced Angelo, who, she believes, ordered the execution of her brother, despite having (or so he thinks) had sex with her:

> Sweet Isabel, do yet but kneel by me.
> Hold up your hands; say nothing: I'll speak all –
> They say best men are moulded out of faults
> And for the most become much more the better
> For being a little bad. So may my husband.
> O Isabel, will you not lend a knee?
>
> (5.1.435–40)

And so here, Isabella, the object of Angelo's grotesque proposal, the novice and the grieving sister of the wrongly executed Claudio, is forced to decide what to do. In this critical moment, a moment when we can hear a whole new way of thinking (one of Brecht's 'useful junction points'), Isabella kneels and begs the Duke to have mercy on her abuser. But, even then, the Duke refuses to reveal the truth ('Your suit's unprofitable: stand up, I say', 5.1.453) and, again, stretches our patience. For it is only when Isabella is confronted with the fact that her brother is still alive (489) that she can understand what has happened, and appreciate what it is that she has learnt.

Many understandably feel uncomfortable at the way that the Duke suggests marriage (492) and Isabella's views are ignored. Indeed, modern directors and actresses have often cited Isabella's silence as clear evidence of Shakespeare's ineluctable sexism, a perfect case study in Benjamin's 'documents in barbarism', and do everything they can to make it speak, usually to suggest Isabella's reluctance. Certainly, working within the Brechtian tradition, this is a moment that needs careful unpacking.

There is, however, another way of looking at this which depends on a close tracking of Isabella's story. We should recall that when we first meet her she is urging 'a more strict restraint' (1.4.4) on the (legendarily strict) Sisterhood of St Clare; we should then notice the way she responds to Lucio's request that she helps her brother, first helplessly ('Alas, what poor ability's in me / To do him good?' 1.4.75), then full of confidence that she'll succeed; we should remember how in her two meetings with Angelo (2.2.20–164 and 2.4.18–187) her assurance grows and she experiences the pleasure of advocacy; we should then note the misery of her visit to her brother in prison (3.1.48–158), the encounter with the grieving Mariana (4.1.48–57) and her acceptance of the duplicity of the 'bed trick' (4.1.64-74); and finally we should observe her acquiescence to Mariana's request to beg for mercy for her abuser (5.1.441). When her story is detailed like this, in all its twists and turns, its ups and downs, we start to see it as a journey from self-imposed ignorance to painfully acquired knowledge, from self-absorption to broader awareness, and, quite possibly, from nun-like chastity to the life-giving potential of marriage, finally triggered by the seeming miracle of her brother's survival.

The Brechtian would argue that *Measure for Measure* dramatizes a society in a process of change, one where the rulers are imposing arbitrary restrictions on their subjects' private lives but whose outcome is not yet clear; what's more, this is being delivered by men subject to the same frailties as their subjects. But Shakespeare also shows that the people of Vienna have their own view of sexuality, whether the cynical exploitation embodied by Mistress Overdone and Pompey or the retreat from the natural world demanded by Isabella's Catholic nuns and Angelo's Puritan self-denial. Thus, Shakespeare hints that there *is* a way of being human beyond such social deformation, and the play, done well, suggests the possibility of justice and human rights.

In other words, the Brechtian director would engage with the many problems embodied in this famously problematic play, while also observing how a careful playing of its actions, its shifting tones and genres, its sophisticated dialectical patterning and its many realistic touches can create something which is strikingly alive and capable of casting light on our own equally problematic times.

Provocations, Exercises and Practical Suggestions

- Read 1.2 of *Measure for Measure* aloud and identify its dramatic inconsistencies. Create additional text (either written by you or from elsewhere in Shakespeare) to explain the impact of the closure of the brothels on those who work in them. Is it possible to do this in such a way that it avoids both prurience and moral condemnation?
- Ask one of the actors to present a short summary of the Duke's journey through the play. Encourage him to show clearly how often his plans don't work out the way he thought they would, how much he has to improvise and the extent to which he is a failure. And then write an epilogue for the Duke, explaining what he has learnt.
- Ask another actor to imagine an alternative story: a tyrant who runs roughshod over everyone, doesn't hand over to a deputy and gives peremptory orders to achieve his aims. Imagine what would happen to Vienna under such leadership.
- Hold a debate with your group and ask them to vote on the following question: Should Isabella sleep with Angelo to save her brother's life, or should Claudio die to protect his sister's honour? Explore what factors might affect the way that they vote, and what would it take for them to change their mind.

- Track Isabella's story and see where it expresses the #MeToo movement's core messages. Look through the text for useful quotes and consider using them in a social media campaign, but also identify those moments where Isabella would find the modern world and its values alien, and vice versa.
- Explore Margot Heinemann's comment about Mariana's poverty and see how it could affect the way that the character is played.
- Imagine that Claudio and Isabella are twins, the sole children of two dead parents from the ruling elite of Vienna, and consider how that might shape their story? What would be the forces shaping them? Dramatize the voices in their head.
- Ask an actor to improvise the diary of the Provost, from first escorting Claudio to prison up to the end of the play. Imagine that he feels strongly that Claudio shouldn't be executed and share his private thoughts about what he sees going on in the prison and help explain why he feels so uncomfortable in disobeying Angelo's commands, but also what it is that wins him over. Now imagine a Provost who is disgusted by extramarital sex and feels that something must be done. Explain how both perspectives are possible within a single figure.
- Write a short epilogue for Isabella. Let it express what she has learnt and what you hope the audience might learn.

King Lear

A Nation in Crisis

Brecht never attempted *King Lear*. He admired a famous production at the State Yiddish Theatre in Moscow in the 1930s but there are surprisingly few references to the play in his writings. It's a shame because it – along with *Coriolanus* – is the most obviously Brechtian of the plays and well suited to a Brechtian approach.

King Lear is, by any reckoning, an intensely political play, which dramatizes many of the underlying conflicts of Early Modern England, especially the fading of the great nobility and the rise of a new aspirational class. But it also hints at the imposition of an increasingly centralizing (Anglican) nation state on the residual forces of (Catholic) resistance, and we can detect in the text a questioning of the vast disparities in wealth and power of Jacobean England. Above all, it enacts a deeply destructive clash within the ruling elite and shows the impact of that on the rest of the country.

These divisions are deepened by an alliance of ruthless individuals within the court (Goneril, Regan and Cornwall) with a number of upwardly mobile outsiders (Edmund, Oswald and Edmund's Captain). These, then, are opposed by other members of the elite, who are driven into exile – whether abroad (Cordelia) or into lower-class disguise (Kent and Edgar) – but also by a growing party of working people (the Fool and various servants and soldiers). The two old men at the centre, the Earl of Gloucester and Lear himself, are the figures responsible for this crisis, but they're also the ones on whom its violence is first inflicted.

The Brechtian director would want to show up the nature of these conflicting forces. It wouldn't be enough to psychoanalyse the central figures, they'd want to clarify how they enact broader belief systems – 'the new family relationships' as Brecht called them – often within a single action (J, 1993, 384). They would want to stage Goneril and Regan's portioning out of their daughterly duties in such a way that an audience caring for its own elderly parents might recognize, while also suggesting the appalling dead end to which such numerical rationing leads; similarly, they would ensure that Edmund, in his questioning of his inferior status as an illegitimate 'bastard', appeals to our own meritocratic impulses, while also observing the savage way he manipulates his credible father and brother, and jostles with increasing brutality for betterment. In other words, they would want the audience to see how the contradictions of society are played out within the individuals, and glimpse their consequences.

The Brechtian director would listen carefully to the voice of Lear's Fool and see to what extent he offers visionary, politicized warnings about the future direction of the kingdom. They would heed Marxists such as Victor Kiernan who wrote that 'from this voice of the people we hear things that swell the chorus of indignation at social evils and upper-class vice and folly' (Kiernan, 1996, 111), or Margot Heinemann, who compared him to 'an iconoclastic, egalitarian, anti-Popish champion of the poor' (1992, 81). In doing so, they would consider the limits of the license that the Fool enjoys and – by extension – the real-life censorship under which Shakespeare himself was working. They would then (perhaps with subtle additions, probably with careful cuts) aim to ensure that this political critique was carefully articulated.

Consequently, the director would also highlight Gloucester's insistence that 'distribution should undo excess, / And each man have enough' (4.1.73-4), and ensure that the audience was aware of the circumstances that lead the King to utter his powerful prayer to the 'poor naked wretches' (3.4.28–36). After all, as Heinemann suggests, 'If Shakespeare was as anti-egalitarian as the [Conservative] Chancellor [Nigel Lawson], how did he come to write *King Lear*, where both Lear and Gloucester realize too late that the wealth of the rich should have been shared with the poor, of whose sufferings they have taken too little care?' (1994, 227). The politically aware director would relish this question.

By carefully registering the contempt shown by so many of the ruling elite for those who work for them, and showing how the breaking down of personal connections leads to an increasingly instrumental attitude to the 'masses', the Brechtian director would help to both historicize the play and sense its contemporary resonance. The director would need to be careful not to sentimentalize the past, but they could suggest how the play dramatizes a profound shift in class relations, leading within a generation to the execution of the King and the emergence of groups committed to 'turning the world upside down'. Little could be more resonant or radical than that.

Cast sizes are often limited in the modern theatre. The danger is that by cutting down on numbers we end up sacrificing the broader political perspective. But Shakespeare's Jacobean company the King's Men also had limited means and, done carefully, a full range of voices can be heard. What the director needs to avoid is investing the leading figures with so much explanatory stage action that the balance of our attention is altered. Everyone on the stage should be of interest.

Above all, the Brechtian director would celebrate the presence of the common people and see the real-life impact of the destructive behaviour of their so-called 'betters'. As the great Russian filmmaker Grigori Kozintsev reminds us:

> Lear is not only the drama of a particular group of people who are linked by the plot, but also a stream of history. Whole structures of life, social situations are carried along and tumbled together. Not only single voices are heard in the din of tragedy... but combined and mighty ensembles, whole choruses. It is not Edgar pretending to be a beggar in order to hide from his pursuers, but poverty itself – the bitter village woe – which howls, laments, treads the earth's surface with nowhere to shelter, no strength to endure.
> (Kozintsev, 1977, 11)

The Impact of the Mighty

It is often said that *King Lear* is a uniquely cruel play, but the Brechtian director – alert to the nuances of historical change – would set out to show the way that the cruelty develops. It's a common mistake in the theatre to present a world of arbitrary violence from the outset, ruled by an absolutist King who is 'mad' from the beginning. Instead, as the text suggests, audiences should observe the workings of a relatively sophisticated society, more a portrait of Jacobean England than a dystopian hellscape, where basic decencies – at least within the ruling elite – are taken for granted. This would allow for a precise charting of the process of moral degeneration that the play dramatizes so brilliantly. As always in the Brechtian theatre, it's change which must be shown, not stasis.

We might start with the opening scene (1.1). It is often assumed that Lear divides his kingdom according to the extent to which his three daughters declare their love for him, with the one who protests the most getting the best part. But a close reading shows that Lear has *already* decided that his eldest daughter, Goneril, will get the north, his second, Regan, will inherit the west, and the richest area (London and the southeast) will be given to his youngest (and favourite), Cordelia. The Brechtian director would make that crystal clear.

Furthermore, even as we observe Lear's fundamental error (you cannot measure love), the Brechtian director would want to show that Lear is also ignoring the basic principles of traditional primogeniture by which the entire estate is inherited by the eldest. Thus, like many of Shakespeare's 'great individuals', Lear's actions cause their own historic agony: the crucial thing – made evident, perhaps, in the onlookers' reactions – is that Lear is doing something radical, but radically dangerous. Such contradictions are the stuff of the Brechtian theatre, and of history.

Brecht wanted audiences to follow the action of this scene with a degree of objectivity (although, ironically, he too seems to have missed the details):

> You can present the famous opening scene in Lear, where he divides his kingdom between his daughters according to the measure of their love for him and gets the measure quite wrong, in such a way that the spectator says: 'He's going about it the wrong way. If only he hadn't said that, or had noticed this, or at any rate thought twice.'
>
> (*BoP*, 2014, 58)

Fascinated by the way that meaning in the theatre is embodied in material objects, Brecht suggested that the King should tear up the map and distribute the relevant parts accordingly:

> Lear could toss the pieces to his daughters in the hope of securing their love that way. And if he took the third piece, the one meant for Cordelia and tore it in half again to give to the other two daughters, that would be a particularly good way of making the spectators stop and think.
>
> (*BoP*, 2014, 91–2)

As ever, 'the truth is concrete'.

The Brechtian director would aim to show the impact of Lear's actions not just on his family but also on his subjects: 'The spectators at the Globe who three centuries ago saw King Lear give away his kingdom in pieces, pitied honest Cordelia who didn't get one of the pieces, not the thousands of people who were thus given away.' Importantly, Brecht adds that 'we ourselves even now scarcely make any protest about the way we are treated' and our objection to the injustice of the first scene should inspire rage about real-life injustices. Indeed, as Margot Heinemann argues, 'to feel its full impact we have to be aware of Lear as patriarch, father, feudal monarch, maddened by a defiance he has never been taught to expect from Lear's point of view, or even from Kent's or Cordelia's (that is from within the society) but from our own, which does not accept the whims of princes as sacred' (1994, 240). It's quite a stretch, but not impossible.

Brecht hints at exactly this in describing Charles Laughton reading the play aloud in Santa Monica:

> He brings out the Lear of the first act excellently, insisting on 10 pounds of filial love per 1000 square metres of land. Then, after he has relinquished his power, the refusal to give up its appurtenances. He contrasts the empty, formal appeal to supernatural powers beautifully with simple, realistic utterances and genuine feelings.
>
> (*J*, 1993, 321)

This attention to detail, and the way that these realistic touches stand in counterpoint to Lear's invocations of 'the terrors of the earth', goes to the heart of his agony in the first half of the play.

Embracing the Poor

The Brechtian director would remember that *King Lear* is more than simply a royal and aristocratic affair.

Thus, they would attend to why the loyal Earl of Kent assumes the disguise of a common man. Is it a heroic sacrifice for the good of everyone or an act of slavish loyalty which fails to engage with the broader catastrophe that Lear's folly has triggered? It's not entirely clear what Kent means by his hope that his 'good intent / May carry through itself to that full issue / For which I razed my likeness' (1.4.2–4), but the action of the play shows that his self-induced humiliation (thirty days in the wilderness, perhaps?) offers the old King essential care and support. The director could even find a way of dramatizing the nature of that care, particularly pertinent against the background of the current care crisis. It's the first suggestion of aristocratic resistance to emerging dictatorship.

One of the services that the disguised Kent offers is to protect the old King, and in 1.4, we see how he deals with Goneril's manservant, the upwardly mobile Oswald. Brecht approaches this episode in a typically dialectical fashion, which encourages us to see it from as many different perspectives as possible:

> THE DRAMATURG What you can't have is the spectators, even those who happen to be servants themselves, taking Lear's side to such an extent that they cheer when a servant is beaten for carrying out his master's orders, as happens in the fourth scene of Act I.
>
> THE ACTOR How can we stop that from happening?
>
> THE DRAMATURG He could still get beaten, but he could be badly injured by the beating and crawl out showing every sign of being in great pain. That would change the mood.
>
> THE ACTOR Then you'd have people turning against Lear for a reason that dates from very recent times.
>
> THE DRAMATURG Not if you're consistent about it. You could show the little band of servants attending the king everybody has rejected, and how they can't get a square meal anywhere anymore and pursue Lear with silent reproaches. The sight of them would surely torment him, and that would provide

a good justification for his rage. You just need to depict the feudal conditions.

(*BoP*, 2014, 91)

Likewise, the Brechtian director would notice how the Fool mocks the disguised Kent for 'taking one's part that's out of favour' (1.4.98) and hear his cynical, if realistic view that 'truth's a dog that must to kennel' (1.4.109).

They might also clarify the conflict between Kent's earthy notions of service and Oswald's more sophisticated manner (brilliantly caught in Kent's tirade against this 'three-suited-hundred-pound, filthy, worsted-stocking knave', 2.2.15–16), but also show the way that Kent's loyalty simply earns him the further humiliation of being put into the stocks (148). This is not just a conflict between 'good' and 'evil': it is, as Brecht would have insisted, a clash between two different ways of thinking, embodied in precisely embodied class conflict.

Then, exploring Edmund's refusal to be hedged in by tradition, along with Oswald's defiance of the old hierarchies, the Brechtian director would do well to see how ambivalent these qualities are. As Brecht brilliantly put it, 'from the bourgeois standpoint all barriers of a feudal nature prove to be fatal and the new attitude triumphs by virtue of its indifference to death in the face of the satisfaction which that attitude offers' (*J*, 1993, 384). In other words, there's something heroic about such radical defiance, however destructive, and the audience should be presented with this powerful contradiction.

The Brechtian director would also pay close attention to Edgar's decision to disguise himself as Poor Tom, who, like an increasing number of people in Jacobean England, survives by begging for alms in the face of ever more stringent controls on indigence. His is an elaborate performance, and Edgar describes his transformation in detail:

>   Whiles I may scape
> I will preserve myself, and am bethought
> To take the basest and most poorest shape
> That ever penury in contempt of man
> Brought near to beast. My face I'll grime with filth,

> Blanket my loins, elf all my hair in knots
> And with presented nakedness outface
> The winds and persecutions of the sky.
> The country gives me proof and precedent
> Of Bedlam beggars, who, with roaring voices
> Strike in their numbed and mortified bare arms
> Pins, wooden pricks, nails, sprigs of rosemary;
> And with this horrible object, from low farms,
> Poor pelting villages, sheepcotes and mills,
> Sometimes with lunatic bans, sometime with prayers,
> Enforce their charity.
>
> (2.2.176–91)

If the director takes this literally, as Brecht would insist, it can make a powerful impact, for the perspective of a figure from the lowest of the low 'alienates' the behaviour of his betters. Modern audiences will struggle with the more obscure references and some passages should probably be cut, but if Poor Tom is a 'holy innocent', a visionary Christ-like figure bearing witness to a set of radical and excluded values, his presence beside his blinded father – and his determination that he shouldn't give into despair – gains in power and political resonance.

The director should also remember the impact of disguise on Kent and Edgar themselves. By experiencing what 'wretches feel' (3.4.34), by 'alienating' themselves from their own privilege and status, they (like so many of Shakespeare's leaders) stand a chance of being able to govern properly. And while the closing moments ache with loss and pain, the final image of Kent and Edgar (5.3.320-5), the two men whose experiences of internal exile have taught them what really matters, offers at least a hint of a better future.

Violence and Hope

The Brechtian director would want to stage the blinding of Gloucester carefully (3.7.22–96). The scene starts with the Duke of Cornwall ordering his three servants to 'Go seek the traitor Gloucester; / Pinion him like a thief, bring him before us' (22–3). Slow to co-operate, it's possible that they've heard their mistress

Regan's advice to 'Hang him instantly!' or her sister Goneril's to 'Pluck out his eyes'; or maybe they're just terrified. Certainly, as the two princesses fight for their victim's attention, they stand there in silence, appalled by this breach of aristocratic unity and royal obligation. Gloucester appeals to his tormenters' humanity, but in reply to his prophecy that he will see 'the winged vengeance overtake such children' (65), Cornwall orders his servants to tip the old man's chair over: they obey, if unwillingly, and the Duke gouges out one of Gloucester's eyes with his heel.

It's at this moment, however, that, in an act of extraordinary courage, the First Servant pleads with his master:

I have served you ever since I was a child,
But better service have I never done you
Than now to bid you hold.

(3.7.72–4)

He snaps at Regan's provocations – 'If you did wear a beard upon your chin, / I'd shake it on this quarrel' (75–6) – and, in the fight that follows, her logic betrays her aristocratic brutality as she kills him, quite possibly from behind. His last words do Gloucester no favours, simply provoking Cornwall into tearing out the remaining eye, but the Duke has been mortally wounded and he staggers off stage, clinging onto his wife and barking orders to his appalled servants. It's a marvellously rich scene that firmly belongs in the Brechtian repertoire.

The eminent Shakespearean James Shapiro named the First Servant as the character in all Shakespeare that he's most drawn to. He is, Shapiro declared (BBC Radio 4, 24 March 2016), a perfect example of the way the playwright 'invests as much in his minor characters as in his great ones'. He knows not to overstep but 'cannot hold back his anger' and, in his willingness 'to speak truth to power' earns himself 'one of the most noble and powerful deaths in Shakespeare'. And so, as Brecht would have insisted, this servant's act of violent rebellion is a turning point, for it saves the country from an even worse fate. A Brechtian production would focus on what it takes for an anonymous servant to do this, and dramatize his moment of choice as vividly as possible. For, like all of us, this Servant could simply have stayed silent in the face of atrocity. And certainly, when done well, audiences are delighted that Cornwall's rampages have been stopped. Thus, the First Servant alienates the Duke's actions, and allows us to see that they can be prevented.

The great Russian film director Grigori Kozintsev described this episode as a 'confusion of movement, stamping of feet and muttered curses' which exposes the danger of unchecked power among the ruling elite (Kozinstev, 1977, 83). But it also shows the limits to mere obedience and the way that an unnamed servant can change the course of history. By bringing an obscure 'bit part' into the foreground, Shakespeare offers a realistic analysis – a distinctly Brechtian analysis, indeed – of the way that violence corrupts, but also suggests that violence may be needed to prevent something worse. The audience will discover that resistance to tyranny is possible, so long as decent people are prepared to do something about it.

In this spirit the Brechtian director should also attend to the moment when Cornwall's remaining servants decide to help the blinded Gloucester:

> 2 SERVANT
> I'll never care what wickedness I do
> If this man comes to good.
> 3 SERVANT   If she live long
> And in the end meet the old course of death,
> Women will all turn monsters.
> 2 SERVANT
> Let's follow the old Earl and get the bedlam
> To lead him where he would. His roguish madness
> Allows itself to anything.
> 3 SERVANT
> Go thou: I'll fetch some flax and whites of eggs
> To apply to his bleeding face. Now heaven help him!
> (3.7.91–106)

This episode is sometimes cut (it's not in the Folio) but it suggests an alternative to aristocratic brutality and these two lowly figures suggest a better future. They certainly should be given the dignity that they deserve.

The Brechtian director would then want to attend to the anonymous Old Man who starts out with Gloucester on his journey to Dover. Their brief dialogue shows something of a world that has disappeared, where the connections between the classes were (supposedly) moral rather than commercial. It's a fine example of Brecht's 'useful junction points':

> OLD MAN   O my good lord, I have been your tenant, and your father's tenant these fourscore years –
> GLOUCESTER
> Away, get thee away; good friend, be gone.
> Thy comforts can do me no good at all,
> Thee they may hurt.
> OLD MAN   Alack, sir, you cannot see your way.
> GLOUCESTER
> I have no way, and therefore want no eyes:
> I stumbled when I saw.
>
> (4.1.14–21)

The Edwardian director Harley Granville Barker unwittingly discovered alienation in this episode: 'Close following the transcendent scenes of Lear's madness and the extreme brutality of the blinding comes this interlude of servant and peasant, of common humanity in its bravery and charity with its simple stumbling talk' (Granville Barker, 1993, 107). Thus, the two affect our view of the other. The Earl is handed over to his son Edgar disguised as Poor Tom, a mad beggar, but this old man is the real thing, one of the millions whose lives are being turned upside down by the chaos that surrounds them. As one insightful critic argued, with this scene 'the common people have come, for a time at least, to occupy the stage' (O'Toole, 2002, 126). The Brechtian would welcome it.

In the action that follows, an image of the huge gulf between rich and poor comes into focus. Handing over his purse to Poor Tom, the Earl of Gloucester utters the simplest formulation of the need for social justice and a more equal society:

> So distribution should undo excess
> And each man have enough.
>
> (4.1.73-4)

Shakespeare, it seems, has done Brecht's work already.

Finally, the Brechtian director would consider the end of the play. In many ways it feels apocalyptic, a landscape of universal death in which even Cordelia must die. But Brecht's Dramaturg admires the domestic quality of the writing:

> Take the scene where Lear dies! That line 'Pray you, undo this button: thank you, Sir'. A wish fights its way through his curses, life has become unbearable, and on top of that his clothes are too tight; it was a king who lives, a man who dies, he is very polite ('thank you, Sir'). The subject is fully dealt with, both broadly and in detail. A disappointed man is dying: dying and disappointment are shown, but don't quite coincide. No forgiveness is granted, but kindnesses are accepted. The man has gone too far, the dramatist does not. Lear's destruction is complete, there is a startling last demonstration of death as a special horror, Lear really does die.
>
> (*BoP,* 2014, 78)

Typically, such acute psychological realism is accompanied by sober political realism. That is, Lear, his daughters, the Fool, Cornwall, Gloucester and Edmund are all dead and it is left to the survivors, the few who adopted a disguise and resisted tyranny, hardened and wise, to imagine the future. The surviving opponents of Hitler might have felt the same, surveying the ruins of Berlin:

> The weight of this sad time we must obey,
> Speak what we feel, not what we ought to say.
> The oldest hath borne most; we that are young
> Shall never see so much, nor live so long.
>
> (5.3.322–5)

We would have to dig deep at such a moment for what Barack Obama dubbed the 'audacity of hope', but it must be possible. After all, mere pessimism leaves us with nothing.

Adapting and Cutting the Text

How much does the text of *King Lear* need to be changed to work in the modern theatre?

The Philosopher in *The Messingkauf Dialogues* is strikingly relaxed on the subject, insisting that 'the play contains an account of the way people lived together long ago' and 'you just need to complete it':

> THE DRAMATURG Many people think such plays should be produced just as they are, and say it's barbaric to make any changes to them at all.
>
> THE PHILOSOPHER But it's a barbaric play. Of course, you need to go about things very carefully so as not to spoil its beauty. If you're going to perform it in accordance with the new rules, so that the spectators don't empathise completely with the king, you can stage nearly the whole play with only minor additions to keep the spectators using their reason.
>
> (*BoP*, 2014, 9)

My own experience in 2002 showed me that so long as the production charts the behaviour of the ruling elite accurately, and shows the other characters realistically, the audience's response is genuinely dialectical, and all the better for being so. Thus, Lear is increasingly wilful, narcissistic and dictatorial just as his physical, political and psychological powers are fading: we empathize with him in his descent into madness while simultaneously noting that his actions are not just self-destructive, they have a destructive impact on his entire country. Similarly, observing Gloucester's story, we admire his loyalty to the King and are appalled by the violence he experiences at the hands of Cornwall and Regan, while also noticing how easily he is duped by his illegitimate son; we might even remember that blindness is the traditional punishment for lust and that Gloucester's folly is all too human. None of this requires much in the way of alterations to the text but it does benefit from an analytical and unsentimental approach.

A good example is the moment when Edmund, having defeated the French, is confronted by what to do with his royal prisoners. He addresses an unnamed Captain, hands him a sealed note, and appeals to his self-interest:

> If thou dost
> As this instructs thee, thou dost make thy way
> To noble fortunes. Know thou this, that men

Are as the time is; to be tender-minded
Does not become a sword. Thy great employment
Will not bear question: either say thou'lt do't,
Or thrive by other means.

(5.3.29–34)

The Captain's reply is unequivocal ('I'll do't, my lord'), and when Edmund insists that he carry out his orders precisely, he goes to the heart of the matter:

I cannot draw a cart, nor eat dried oats.
If it be man's work, I'll do't.

(5.3.39–40)

We could interpret this as the speech of a man who has lost his humanity. But it's also an understandable response to an aristocrat offering him a unique opportunity to better himself, while threatening to let him 'thrive by other means' (sack him) if he refuses. Everyone, the episode shows, has his price and we should pause before condemning the Captain for his moral failures. It's a perfect example of alienation in practice.

In other words, it's not that *King Lear* needs extensive rewriting; it's that careful attention needs to be paid to the text. And when we do that, we'll find that the 'complex seeing', the dialectical perspectives, the 'alienation effect' itself, will look after themselves: they're deep in the texture of the play. As Brecht once joked, 'Give me an intelligent model of *King Lear*, and I will find my fun in recreating it' (*BoT*, 1964, 224). Maybe the play itself could have done that for him?

Peter Brook and Grigori Kozintsev

In thinking about *King Lear*, the Brechtian director would do well to watch the film of Peter Brook's mighty 1962 RSC production with Paul Scofield. Brook was much influenced by two essays: Wilson Knight's '*King Lear* and the Comedy of the Grotesque' and Jan Kott's '*King Lear* or *Endgame*'. Both explored the extent to which Shakespeare's great tragedy communicates absurdity, where dignity, kindness and human decency have no place. Brook's production was irredeemably bleak, set in a no-man's land with many of the characters dressed in rags. It reminded some of the stripped back aesthetic of *Mother Courage*, but, with his roots in existentialism, Brook – who had wanted to direct at the Berliner Ensemble – worked in an entirely non-Brechtian fashion.

One notable example was Brook's decision to follow the Folio and cut the short scene following the blinding of Gloucester when Cornwall's two surviving servants express their opposition to their master and set out to help the blinded Earl. In Brook's production, Margot Heinemann tells us, 'the world of Lear [was] shown as wholly, unchangeably (not relatively) black and evil, and so the crucial turning point, when the oppressed common people begin to resist the bullies and torturers, has to go – which means the forces which, however feeble as yet, will one day alter this world have to go too' (1994, 247). Indeed, as a younger critic insists, 'without this, the play has no corrective to its own cruelties' (Smith, 2020, 236).

The essential point is that Shakespeare both plumbs the depths of human depravity *and* shows the possibility of change. And so, much more Brechtian in spirit is Kozintsev's magnificent film of the play with its epic portrayal of the impact of aristocratic and royal dysfunction on the entire population. Kozintsev offers the ultimate answer to Brook's 'empty space' when he declares in his diary, 'There is no "desert" in *Lear*, the world of tragedy is densely populated' (Kozintsev, 1977, 82). A Brechtian production would show something similar.

Provocations, Exercises and Practical Suggestions

- Stage the first scene of *King Lear* using only a single chair, a crown and a map of England. Do what you can to ensure that the audience understands that Lear has already decided that Cordelia will be given the richest parts. Experiment with Brecht's suggestion that Lear should tear the map into three as he divides the nation. And explore the implication of the moment when he hands his crown to the dukes of Cornwall and Albany and tells them to 'part' it between them. Track the reactions of the onlookers

to all this, understand what they are thinking but also the extent to which they do not dare express their thoughts.
- Chart the shifts in Lear's *gests* in the first scene of the play and experiment with how those can be embodied physically.
- Highlight those moments in the play when (1) Lear and Gloucester's words and deeds are foolish and counterproductive and (2) when decent people respond critically to them or to the behaviour of those eager to exploit their folly.
- Read the Fool's speeches and highlight his criticism of his betters. But also consider the limits of his license and work how to show that he thinks more than he says. Ask the actor to rephrase his comments with 'Instead of [saying something very forceful] the Fool [cracks a joke/sings a song or whatever], smuggling in a hidden meaning so as to avoid being punished'.
- Write diaries for Kent and Edgar which explain why they go into disguise, and how their experiences prepare them for what the end of the play suggests.
- Discuss ways of ensuring that the play is the story of a country as well as of two families, and consider what the play would look like with 100 actors, but also how to make an impact with only 15?
- Consider how the audience can be helped to consider the lives of the 'poor naked wretches' and whether Gloucester's conclusion that 'distribution should undo excess, / And each man have enough' could be made resonant today.
- Rehearse the scene of Gloucester's blinding and explore how to give the First Servant the space and attention that he deserves.
- Peter Brook staged *King Lear* as an image of human futility. Discuss how it could suggest the 'audacity of hope' instead?

Coriolanus

The Citizens' Revolt

With its vivid dramatization of class struggle and the downfall of a charismatic leader, *Coriolanus* inevitably appealed to Brecht. The conflict between the warlike hero and the plebeians made it especially resonant in post-war Germany, morally, socially and culturally devastated by the twelve long years of Hitler's dictatorship. But Brecht's interest in *Coriolanus* predated the Third Reich: in 1917 he hailed it as 'wonderful!' and excitedly described Eric Engel's 1925 Berlin production as 'a model of the director's art' which was 'decisively important in the emergence of the Epic Theatre' (Barnett, 2013, 114).

The play opens (1.1.1–246) with a group of Roman 'citizens' gathering to protest against the rising price of corn as a result of the patricians stockpiling it for their own profit. But who are these people? The Marxist (and Brechtian) would see them as 'plebeians', a projection of the emerging proletarian masses of Early Modern England, and urban cousins to the peasants caught up in the large-scale Midlands Revolt of May 1607. Indeed, their complaints would have struck a familiar chord in Jacobean London, described by one historian as a 'congested, polarized and angry city' lying at 'the heart of a war-torn, over-taxed and now hunger-threatened nation' (Fitter, 2012, 145):

We are accounted poor citizens, the patricians good. What authority surfeits on would relieve us. If they would yield us but the superfluity while it were wholesome, we might guess they relieved us humanely. But they think we are too dear. The leanness that afflicts us, the object of our misery, is as an inventory to particularize their abundance; our sufferance is a gain to them.

(1.1.13–20)

Has political grievance ever been so forcefully expressed in classical drama?

We should, however, heed the observation in Peter Holland's 2013 Arden edition that the designation 'citizens' merely means people who live in the city, who are not necessarily plebeians. But while this may disappoint those who see the scene as an example of naked class conflict, it has its own political nuance: after all, if the *citizens* are protesting about the price of food, the state really is in trouble. What's essential is that the City of Rome is embodied in these 'citizens', of whatever trade or status.

In thinking about *Coriolanus* in post-war Berlin, Brecht was keen to ensure that the audience takes these protestors seriously. Indeed, he was shrewd enough to insist that they shouldn't be portrayed as 'an unqualifiedly progressive, strongly class-conscious proletariat' (Barnett, 2013, 145). And, in a fascinating parenthesis, he was typically astute about the representation of such grievance:

> As far as Shakespeare's 'hatred of the plebs' is concerned, it may well be that [the great Danish critic and Shakespearean] Brandes is right and he was putting his English class comrades on the stage instead of Roman plebeians – not necessarily because he got mixed up, but more probably because he was more interested in Londoners than in Romans – but applying a theatrical rod to the back of the common man need not, as Brandes thinks, derive from snobbish hatred.
>
> (*J*, 1993, 434)

It's unsurprising that this opening scene should provide us with perhaps the most probing of Brecht's commentaries on Shakespeare. Hailed by the eminent American critic and philosopher Stanley Cavell as *Coriolanus*' 'most compelling political interpretation', Brecht's insights take the form of a dialogue between four unspecified 'collaborators'. They start with a brisk exposition of Shakespeare's intentions:

B. How does the play begin?
R. A group of plebeians has armed itself with a view to killing the patrician Caius Marcius, an enemy to the people, who is opposed to lowering the price of corn. They say that the plebeians' sufferance is the patricians' gain.
B. ?
R. Have I left something out?
B. Are Marcius' services mentioned?
R. And disputed.
P. So you think the plebeians aren't all that united? Yet they loudly proclaim their determination.
W. Too loudly. If you proclaim your determination as loudly as that it means that you are or were undetermined and highly so.
(*BoT*, 1964, 252)

P. then alludes to the condescending way these characters are usually performed. B., however, points out how 'hard it is for the oppressed to become united', insisting that 'they are forced to snatch the wretched crumbs from each other's mouths'. The essential point is that 'neither we nor the audience [should] be allowed to overlook the contradictions that are bridged over, suppressed, ruled out, now that sheer hunger makes a conflict with the patricians unavoidable'. What's more, as B. insists, 'This unity of the plebeians will be broken up, so it is best not to take it for granted at the start.' It's a typically wry, 'bottom up' understanding which should encourage us to read the play more carefully.

Then, in considering Menenius' 'world-famous parable' of the belly (1.1.91–158), B. points out that 'Shakespeare gives the plebeians good arguments to come back with.' He also praises as 'lovely stuff' the fact that with the external 'threat', the plebeians fade away. And this admiration of the contradictory realism of Shakespeare's citizens – neither heroes nor villains, fools or particularly wise – is the underlying theme of the entire dialogue. In the theatre, such individuality is all too often submerged by generalized anger. But we should be careful not to take Coriolanus' contempt for the 'many-headed multitude' (2.3.15-6) as a guide: indeed, we mustn't assume that anything a character says, however dominant, is the voice of the playwright, and Brecht's alienation effect, his seeking out of opposing perspectives, prevents that.

The Enemy of the People

Perhaps the chief question a director of *Coriolanus* must answer is how the central figure should be played. The traditional reading sees Martius (his name before his victory at Corioles) as a heroic figure, one of the 'great men' of history, who stands above the mass and is tragically destroyed as a result. He may be arrogant, this argument runs, but this is simply a 'fatal flaw', fundamental to his genius, and the audience should feel sympathy towards him as a result. The Marxist, by contrast, regards him as an 'enemy of the people', whose hatred of the plebeians and reluctance to govern democratically means that his defeat and death is inevitable. In such a reading, *Coriolanus* isn't a tragedy so much as a history play which allows us to draw our own conclusions.

Martius, Brecht argues, thinks he is indispensable, but the problem is that 'everyone is dispensable' (Barnett, 2013, 144). Indeed, Margot Heinemann insisted that a radical production of the play should 'show that no leader, however talented, is indispensable' (1994, 245). 'Coriolanus', she explained, is a 'hero, yes, but one whose pride make him not only an exemplar of Roman virtues but a traitor to his country' (1994, 227). For Brecht, the city of Rome is much more than just one individual ego, and the play dramatizes the irreconcilable conflict between the two:

> The tragedy of the common man naturally interests us less than the one the individual man brings on the community. We must at the same time stay close to Shakespeare if we are not to mobilise all his outstanding qualities against ourselves. So we think it is best to turn the hurt pride of Shakespeare's Coriolanus into another significant attitude not too remote from Shakespeare, namely Coriolanus' belief in his indispensability. This is what brings about his ruin and robs the common weal of a valuable man.
>
> (J, 1993, 434–5)

Thus, Coriolanus' fundamental problem 'is that he continually makes the wrong decisions in a society that indulges his individualism' (Barnett, 2015b, 185). It's something we can recognize in our own populist leaders.

Intriguingly, Brecht was adamant that such a reading should not hinder the satisfaction we take from watching the action: 'We have to get beyond a mere sense of empathy with the hero Marcius [*sic*] in order to achieve a richer form of enjoyment', he insisted. 'We must at least be able to "experience" the tragedy not only of Coriolanus himself but also of Rome, and specifically of the plebs' (*CP*, 2014, 447). What's more, even here, Brecht wanted a dialectical approach and resisted 'the temptation to make Coriolanus a wholly unsympathetic or contemptible militarist'. Instead, 'he has to be shown as a hero who would be valuable to his country if he were not prevented by pride and narrow class outlook' (Heinemann, 1994, 245). It's a typically layered perspective, which puts paid to the idea that Brecht's readings of Shakespeare are simplistic.

Indeed, Brecht dramatizes a profound contradiction: the antisocial leader, who feels nothing but contempt for the mob, manages to lead the people of Rome first to victory, but then on to disaster. He is charismatic, courageous and inspiring, but *also* antisocial, contemptuous and arrogant. What's more, as the American critic Bryan Reynolds explains, his disdain for democratic participation suggests its own theatrical metaphor:

> In his refusal to perform, Coriolanus aligns the audience with the 'common people', thereby disparaging the audience as well. As a result, he sets himself apart physically, morally and spiritually from all people (the characters, the actors, the audience), as so many monarchs and dictators have done throughout history, including those who ruled over Shakespeare and Brecht (James I and Stalin, respectively).
>
> (Reynolds, 2003, 96)

It's an insight that Brecht, with his interest in politics as performance (and performance as politics), would have relished.

Coriolanus is the product of his upbringing, and, in his mother, Shakespeare presents a further contradiction: the dedicated patrician who wills her beloved son to be wounded, even killed in war, so as to uphold the social order that she represents. As such, Volumnia is a ruling-class version of Mother Courage (Helene Weigel, Brecht's definitive Courage, played her superbly) and a Brechtian production would aim to show this as more than a mere psychological quirk; it is fundamental to the perpetuation of her class and privilege.

Exploring the play's first great climax, when Coriolanus is persuaded from sacking Rome, Brecht argued that Shakespeare deliberately 'lowered the tone' in Volumnia's speeches 'in which she opposes her son who is marching against his home city, a speech which he deliberately fashions so that it lacks force'. Brecht 'wanted Coriolanus to be stopped from carrying out his plan, not by real reasons or by being profoundly moved, but by the lethargy with which he succumbs to an old habit' (*BAP*, 2003, 150). This argument (which is frankly hard to justify from Shakespeare's text) supports Brecht's insistence that Coriolanus' sparing of Rome should not be the result of his mother's intervention but rather a rejection of him by the plebeians and their representatives. And Manfred Wekwerth takes this episode as an example of how dramatic surprise can provoke 'interventionist thought': 'Why doesn't Coriolanus, whose mother taught him to stand firm, resist this selfsame mother's plea when to relent will entail certain death?' (Wekwerth, 2012, 63). The classical Shakespearean might point to psychological contradiction as his justification, but Wekwerth prefers to give sole agency to the citizens and their representatives.

The Brechtian director would also want to contrast Volumnia with Coriolanus' young wife, Virgilia, who is appalled by the possibility of losing her husband and her child's father to the war. Such a distinction would show that Volumnia belongs to the old Roman order, in many ways a dying one, in which tenderness and vulnerability are banished. We can see this in the discussion about the upbringing of Coriolanus' son, where Virgilia tries to break the cycle in the face of Volumnia's opposition. This, then, is a perfect example of Brecht's 'junction points', where the values of the new hit up against the old, echoing the historic clash between individualism and public accountability which was increasingly tearing the English body politic apart at the time. Thus, Shakespeare shows that there are contradictions *within* classes as well as between classes.

Coriolanus and *Coriolan*

Brecht started his adaptation in early 1951, and collaborated with Caspar Neher on (unrealized) designs. But when 'the Party leadership decreed it artistically unacceptable to caricature classical works', he mothballed the project, and abandoned it entirely in 1953 (Parker, 2014, 558). Indeed, his adaptation was left unresolved on his death.

In a largely positive analysis, the Canadian critic Robert Ormsby explains that Brecht's *Coriolan* 'is only about 60 percent as long as Shakespeare's and about 17 percent of this material is new' (Ormsby, 2014, 48). Brecht's 'relatively minor' changes, Margot Heinemann explains, are 'first, that the plebeians are more consistent and organised' than in Shakespeare. Thus, Brecht subtly emphasizes their arguments and introduces a 'Man with Child' into the opening scene, who announces that he is going to leave Rome in search of a better future: 'We'll have water, fresh air and a grave. What more is there for us plebeians in Rome? At least we won't have to fight rich men's wars' (*CP*, 2014, 70). Other innovations include borrowing the articulate and quick-thinking Cobbler from *Julius Caesar* (1.1.13–32) and putting him into the scene when Coriolanus solicits the citizens for their votes. Brecht 'always takes pains to depict his proletarians not as humourless fanatics but to equip them with both homespun and gallows humour' (Barnett, 2013, 145), and it is the determination of the common people, led by the tribunes, that ultimately forces Brecht's Coriolanus to 'turn back to his own destruction'.

A second area of change is in the role of the tribunes who, in Shakespeare, are 'shabby politicians who envy Marcius and manipulate the people' (Heinemann, 1994, 246), but become in Brecht the people's spokesmen and genuine leaders. Indeed, they 'provide good advice and act strategically' (Barnett, 2013, 147). As Manfred Wekwerth and Joachim Tenschert pointed out, such an interpretation is closer to Plutarch's account than Shakespeare's (*TDR*, 1967, 113) and 'Menenius, who could be seen in Shakespeare as a reconciler, is here merely a twisty patrician using soft-soap rhetoric' (Heinemann, 1994, 246). Locating Brecht within the context of Communist East Germany, Ormsby intriguingly speculates about the extent to which he uses the tribunes to present 'politically committed artists like himself as "Leninist" representatives of the people, figures who could instruct the workers to become a counterforce to replaceable tyrants like Stalin who jeopardize the future of Marxism' (Ormsby, 2014, 52).

Brecht's most memorable change comes right at the end, when the Senate rejects all requests for Coriolanus to be memorialized, and the last word is a simple 'Rejected'. This is in response to a request that his mother and wife should be allowed to wear mourning in public for ten months. If it feels brutal, an audience that had survived the personality cults of both Hitler and Stalin would have found it appropriate.

The Posthumous Production

In 1960 the East German government finally granted approval for a production of *Coriolan* which, after an 'elephantine gestation period' (Barnett, 2015b, 193), was finally premiered in West Germany in 1962, but not attempted by the Berliner Ensemble until 1964, eight long years after its author's death. Almost 10 per cent of the text was further adapted by Wekwerth and Tenschert, who maintained most of Brecht's core insights, but 'did not want to show the people as "Revoluzzer"' (young people who don't know how to conduct a 'proper' revolution), but as a group that had revolutionary potential once they'd heard a convincing argument (Barnett, 2015b, 184).

Brecht had declared that *Coriolanus* was 'probably the only Shakespeare [play] of any topicality which we can halfway cast' (Parker, 2014, 557), and he wanted the legendary working-class actor Ernst Busch in the title role. By the time the Ensemble came to stage it, the part was taken by the youthful Ekkehard Schall, whose performance as 'a figure who had overplayed his hand, unable to appreciate that the majority of the people only valued him for one particular talent' (Barnett, 2015b, 187), was much praised.

Wekwerth and Tenschert knew that the battle scenes needed careful handling: 'We wanted to show that Coriolanus is an expert in all the technical skills of war and is much needed by his countrymen. He is a very good general, not just a bully-boy' (*TDR*, 1967, 113). The young choreographer Ruth Berghaus (who later ran the Ensemble) went to the heart of the matter: 'We're supposed to be showing how barbaric the fight was and how the different warriors behave differently, not how savage or barbarous our actors can be' (Barnett, 2015b, 186). By all accounts, however, these scenes were unpleasantly loud and protracted, with mass chanting and furious shouts, uncomfortably suggesting the hysteria of the Nazi period, leading some critics to complain of 'theatrical bewitchment', the very opposite of the cool alienation Brecht had strived for. Nevertheless, the photographs of these sequences are among the most striking images of a Brechtian staging, and the 'production is commonly seen as one of the company's most brilliant achievements' (Willett, 1984, 41).

In a fascinating discussion between Wekwerth, Tenschert, Weigel and Schall, it becomes clear that their interpretation was intentionally different from Brecht's, who in 1951 had 'thought of the parallel with fascism'; 'But now', Wekwerth explained, 'experiences with the cult of personality and Stalin force a new reading of the play. We show Coriolanus as a very useful man in the beginning who later exploits his usefulness for purposes of blackmail' (*TDR*, 1967, 113). Ormsby, however, detects in their work, a gradual accommodation of aspects of the 'great man' view of history, partly as a way of being more faithful to Shakespeare's original, but also, perhaps, to please their increasingly doctrinaire (and aesthetically conservative) masters.

In approaching *Coriolanus*, the Brechtian director should also read Günter Grass' satirical drama *The Plebeians Rehearse the Uprising* (1966), which imagines a version of Brecht ('The Boss') directing an adaptation of the play as a parable of proletarian revolt, while simultaneously defending the DDR's suppression of the workers' uprising in June 1953. In reply, we should remember that although Brecht was writing his adaptation at the time, he had to do it in secret. And if his response was controversial, he never actually directed the play and Grass' *jeu d'esprit* is pure hypothesis. It's also revealing that Grass described *Coriolanus* as a 'bothersome play', in which the plebeians, 'like London artisans, are cowardly and ignorant dogs', and his reactionary reading rather colours his negative views of Brecht (Grass, 1966, 9). We should also recall that in the 1960s Jan Kott, a citizen of communist Poland who had renounced his party membership, argued that 'the history that breaks *Coriolanus* is not royal history anymore. It is the history of a city divided into plebeians and patrician. It is the history of class struggle' (Kott, 1964, 147). Brecht's dialectical reading of Shakespeare was perhaps more common than Grass imagined.

'Only Small Changes'

Brecht's work on *Coriolanus* marks the highpoint of his interrogation of Shakespeare. But it also marks his closest and most respectful engagement with the original.

'In *Coriolan*', David Barnett writes, Brecht 'attempts to deal with Shakespeare on his own terms', and what's striking is how modest were his interventions (2013, 144). Indeed, in December 1952, he argued that 'as the feeling for history gets stronger, and when the self-confidence of the masses is greater, it will be possible to leave everything pretty well as it is', adding, intriguingly, that in capitalist West Germany Shakespeare's text could 'be performed just as it is' (*J*, 1993, 452). Then, in the last entry in his *Journal* he declared that, after almost forty years of wrestling with Shakespeare, it should be possible to stage *Coriolanus* without any of his alterations, 'or with very few of them, relying solely on good direction' (*J*, 1993, 460). And, finally, in an interview in 1956, not long before his death, Brecht said that if he was staging the play today, 'it is only small changes I would have to make in the production, changes of emphasis' (Barnett, 2013, 150).

In other words, Brecht came to realize that it might be possible to be 'faithful' to 'the great realist', after all.

Provocations, Exercises and Practical Suggestions

- Identify all the moments when Coriolanus expresses contempt for the plebeians, and improvise a scene of him as a modern politician talking privately to his friends and family about how much he despises the poor.
- Similarly, identify all the moments when he begs the plebeians for their voices and play these as the campaigning of a modern political campaign. Now try letting him say the contemptuous speeches in public: how might the plebeians accept such contempt as part of his appeal.
- Look at the first scene and give each of the citizens an invented name, age, occupation and family background. See how they can be differentiated from each other,

but also what they have in common. Compare their disagreements about tactics with shifts in modern trade unionism: division and change aren't necessarily a sign of incompetence or folly; more likely, it shows that political struggle is complicated and that tactics change according to circumstance.

- Ask your group to read Brecht's dialogue about the first scene aloud and see where it clarifies, but also where it obscures. Flesh out each point with examples from the play and improvisation.
- Devise a monologue of a military leader who thinks he is indispensable, above the law and immune to the usual problems faced by democratic politicians. See what his vulnerabilities might be and invent other figures to show him how wrong he is. Then explore the way he uses an external threat to shore up his position.
- Improvise a debate between Volumnia and Virgilia about the best way to bring up a boy in a world which has traditionally championed physical strength and courage. Is it possible to show that Volumnia has a point, and that Virgilia fails to understand the broader demands of Rome?
- If the director's *fabel* is to show that no one is indispensable, however mighty, how much does the text need to change to communicate that?

The Tempest

'The Freckled Whelp'

There are only a handful of references to Shakespeare's late romance in Brecht's writings, and, to an extent, its fantastical tone feels alien to his earthy materialism. But *The Tempest* can be approached as a theatrical parable, and when staged with the right degree of Brechtian scrutiny, can reveal a series of interconnected and intriguing insights.

The first is into colonialism. It has been argued that *The Tempest* reflects the establishment of the first colonies in North America, and in conceiving of the island, the Brechtian director will want to consider the nature of Prospero's presence there. It's hard to escape the conclusion that as an aristocrat forced into exile he is, de facto, the occupier of someone else's territory. There are many ways of engaging with this question, but a production which simply opted for the consoling beauties of the 'yellow sands' or the play's much vaunted meta-theatricality would fail to engage with its historic contradictions, and so lose its enduring resonance.

Crucial is our approach to Caliban. But who is this mysterious figure? The fact is, he refuses to be pinned down: Is he a courtly projection, a racist encounter with a stereotypical 'other', or a three-dimensional portrait of slavery and oppression? But he's absolutely central to Shakespeare's exploration not just of creativity and the imagination but of exploitation and rebellion too.

There are many decisions to be made, each with political consequences. First, what is Caliban's physical state? The *dramatis personae* describes a 'savage and deformed slave', and Prospero speaks of 'a freckled whelp, hag-born not honoured with / A human shape' (1.2.283–4), but there's no indication of physical disability. Indeed, Prospero and Miranda make him do hard physical labour and there is much to suggest physical strength. We know that the island is his home, that it was stolen from his mother, and that he is involved in a fight for its freedom, but more than that is unclear. The Brechtian director will need to make some decisions here.

Significantly, Caliban doesn't take his mistreatment well and 'defiantly refuses to feel grateful or contrite for the consequences of Prospero's attempts to civilize him' (Ryan, 1995, 132):

> When thou cam'st first
> Thou strok'st me and made much of me; wouldst give me
> Water with berries in't, and teach me how
> To name the bigger light and how the less
> That burn by day and night.
>
> (1.2.333–7)

Furthermore, like the colonized everywhere, Caliban regrets succumbing to his imperial master and is furious at the way that his world has been turned upside down:

> For I am all the subjects that you have,
> Which first was mine own king, and here you sty me
> In this hard rock, whiles you do keep from me
> The rest o' th' island.
>
> (1.2.343–6)

Whether Caliban's attempted rape of Miranda should be regarded as the violent revenge of the oppressed, it's clear that she taught him language – *her* language, of course – whose only benefit, he declares, is that he now knows 'how to curse'.

To confuse things further, Caliban reserves his real rage for the way the spirit world torments him:

> Sometime like apes that mow and chatter at me
> And after bite me, then like hedgehogs which
> Lie tumbling in my barefoot way and mount
> Their pricks at my footfall.
>
> (2.2.9–12)

The Brechtian director would want to ensure that the play's airy reputation doesn't obscure the brutality of Prospero's power, nor the extent of Caliban's suffering. The fact is that Caliban is fired up by 'the passion of resentment' (Auden, 2000, 302) and with good reason too. As one modern critic put it, 'Though an enchanted island, *The Tempest* is no utopia: it is rigidly hierarchical, and its master-servant relationships are stripped of any sense of mutual benefit' (Fitter, 2017, 242). The Brechtian director would embrace this.

Caliban has particular purchase in our (supposedly) postcolonial world and the Brechtian director wouldn't ignore the bitterly distorting experience of slavery on both subject and master, as dramatized so brilliantly in Aimé Césaire's *La Tempête*, in which the slave confronts his colonial master with threats of revolution: 'I know that one day / my bare fist, my bare fist alone / will be enough to crush your world!' (Césaire, 2009, 25–6). Here – as in Shakespeare, and as Brecht would have argued – Caliban's resort to violence simply echoes the violence that has been meted out to him.

Defending Caliban from the dangers of theatrical grotesquery, one critic reminds us that 'Caliban loves music, has learned English, speaks as good poetry as the playtext has to offer, and knows something about the laws of inheritance' (Patterson, 1989, 155), while another insists that we hear in him 'the voice of the dispossessed as powerfully as we ever hear it in literature until the dispossessed themselves come to be heard' (Rosen, 2004, 70). And this apparent contradiction – a brilliantly Brechtian contradiction – between oppression and a feeling for poetry makes for a vividly three-dimensional figure.

Finally, in casting, the Brechtian director would need to consider ethnicity, especially if the play's colonial aspect is to be examined. But so also should they think about Caliban's possible disability: as one academic study pointed out, 'this indigenous islander is doubly disavowed for both disfigurement and nonwhiteness' (Hobgood, 2021, 25). Every possible permutation has been tried, from the self-consciously racial to strict colour blindness and a wide range of disabilities have been shown. In 1991, Peter Brook cast a 'dwarfish' blonde as Caliban (the only white actor on stage), effectively turning the whole question on its head.

Balancing these many demands makes Caliban peculiarly hard to realize in the theatre. This may be a consequence of the metaphorical and literary nature of the play, whose poetry can easily become detached from its dramatic context, but also, perhaps, because Shakespeare's purposes are beyond us. The Brechtian director would, I suggest, be wise to follow the role's many contradictions and let its quirky shape create its own elusive form.

The Ship of State

Although written at the same time as the establishment of the first colonies in the New World, the ostensible setting of *The Tempest* is an island somewhere in the busy sea lanes between Southern Europe and North Africa, the central Mediterranean of Virgil's *Aeneid*, in fact. Of course, with its imaginative and poetic freedom, the text doesn't decisively settle on anywhere and so probably the best we can do is a theatrical abstraction, as elusive as Brecht's Chicago and open to multiple interpretations, even while we explore its many political and social configurations. Thus, Caliban's island (as we should probably call it, as opposed to Prospero's island) is a space in which the Brechtian director will have to make major decisions and those decisions will have consequences.

Even without precise geographical coordinates, however, the play enacts political struggle and social change. Thus, the Brechtian director would want to explore the opening scene (1.1), in which we see the King's ship in grave peril and a lowly boatswain telling his mighty masters what to do. Indeed, as W. H. Auden rhetorically asked, 'Who has authority in the society of a sinking ship?' (2000, 299). This reflects the broader upheavals in the ship of state, storm tossed by the equalising force of nature. Challenged, the Boatswain rhetorically enquires, 'what cares these roarers for the name of king?' (1.1.16–17), ordering the courtiers to return to their cabin and 'trouble us not'. Indeed, he challenges one of them directly:

> If you can command these elements to silence and work peace of the present, we will not hand a rope more. Use your authority! If you cannot, give thanks you have lived so long and make yourself ready in your cabin for the mischance of the hour, if it so hap.
> (1.1.23–26)

The play is just beginning, but the class conflict is palpable.

Gonzalo, however, takes 'great comfort from this fellow', who 'hath no drowning mark upon him' (27–8). And when the others reappear, the Boatswain – abused as a 'bawling, blasphemous, incharitable dog' (39–40) – sets them to work. Despite his best efforts, however, the gentry are in despair. One of them blames the Boatswain, saying he'll 'be hanged yet' (58), but nothing can save the ship, which soon splits on the rocks, and 'faced with the roaring sea, a boatswain means more than a king' (Kott, 1964, 243). Social hierarchy crumbles when confronted by nature's power and a Brechtian director would want to show it.

The director would also need to engage with the political divisions among the shipwrecked aristocrats, and work out how to present Gonzalo's declaration that if he were king of the island, 'All things in common nature should produce / Without sweat of endeavour', insisting that 'nature should bring forth / Of its own kind, all foison, all abundance, / To feed my innocent people' (2.1.160–5). As so often in Shakespeare, political divisions within the ruling class are as important as the divisions between the rulers and the ruled, and Gonzalo's vision of utopia would have to register clearly if the play's broader exploration of confinement, exile and freedom is to be heard.

'Thought Is Free'

The Boatswain and Gonzalo aren't the only political rebels in *The Tempest*, and a key challenge for the Brechtian director is how to present the dreams of freedom expressed not just by Caliban but the shipwrecked butler Stephano and the jester Trinculo. How much of a threat does this trio of working men pose to the ruling elite and how seriously should the audience take them?

Ever the conservative, Coleridge insisted that with these three we 'observe the good nature with which [Shakespeare] seems always to make sport with the passions and follies of a mob, as with an irrational animal' (Bate, 1992, 534), while Auden countered that while they are 'not murderous people', like all failed revolutionaries, they have 'no sense of direction' (Auden, 2000, 302). The text, however, suggests something more nuanced. For 'these fellows with their sea-wit' are 'as like drunken sailors as they can be'

(Hazlitt, 1908, 93), and though their rebellion may be doomed, its revolutionary intent is icily prophetic. A Brechtian director would certainly want to engage with this question.

The jester Trinculo knows all about the struggles poor people like him face: 'When they will not give a doit to relieve a lame beggar, they will lay out ten to see a dead Indian' (2.2.31–2), he comments satirically in a way that the Brechtian director would highlight. But stumbling across Caliban, he expresses the classic European concern about whether non-whites, especially disabled non-whites, were human at all: 'What have we here, a man or a fish? Dead or alive? A fish: he smells like a fish, a very ancient and fish-like smell' (24–5). Nevertheless, cold and alone, he overcomes his snobbery and clambers under Caliban's gabardine, declaring that 'misery acquaints a man with strange bedfellows'. But oversize fish washed up on a beach were traditional omens of political upheaval, and, once Stephano has joined them, they're soon toasting the possibility of freedom. It's class solidarity, of a kind.

Hailing from Naples (the largest city in Europe at the time), Stephano is a resolutely urban figure who demonstrates real courage, particularly in the face of Ariel's trickery. Alcohol is his fatal flaw: when we first see him, he has a bottle in his hand and is singing that he 'shall no more to sea' (2.2.41); when we next see him, he refuses to moderate his consumption. He's the leader of the three, and in this contradictory quality, he reminds us of that earlier rebel, Jack Cade in *Henry VI, Part Two*: hard-drinking and fantastical, but tender and visionary too. 'Thought is free' (3.2.123), he sings eloquently, and, as the three men approach Prospero's cave, Stephano strikes an almost self-consciously Macbeth-like note: 'I do begin to have bloody thoughts' (4.1.220–1).

One of the many Brechtian contradictions is the way that, free of the restraints of society, the old hierarchies endure, in which the jester Trinculo – a member of the 'impoverished English masses' (Hobgood, 2021, 25) – looks down on the non-European slave ('a drunken monster'), while the upwardly mobile butler condescends to them both: it's a typically clear-eyed observation from the 'great realist' which allows us to celebrate their revolutionary spirit while also seeing its fissures and weaknesses. Indeed, Stephano enjoys 'absolute despotism' (Bate, 1992, 534) over the jester, whose commitment to freedom is skin deep: 'reeling ripe', he's more interested in alcohol than politics and, when quizzed by his real master, confesses ruefully, 'I have been in such a pickle since I saw you last, that I fear me will never out of my bones' (5.1.279, 282–3).

So how can the director present all this in the progressive theatre? These men are hardly convincing revolutionaries, whatever the depth of their feeling or resentment at injustice. The best that can be done, I suggest, is to see them as individuals, with different perspectives and life experiences, who, together, make up a vivid class interest. And occasional textual interventions could grant their rebellion more dignity and force than is usually seen, without changing the overall arc of the story, and the play – not my favourite – would survive.

Miranda and Her Father

Finally, of course, the director will need to come to some conclusions about Prospero, his daughter Miranda and her suitor, Ferdinand.

One of the notable things about the early expository scene (1.2) is the depth of Prospero's rage. Certainly, it would be hard for an actor, however charismatic, to play it for straightforward empathy. Instead, we see a seething mass of resentment: this is a powerful man ('the prime Duke, being so reputed / In dignity, and for the liberal arts / Without a parallel', 1.2.72–4) forced into exile by his brother and still angry about it. We're told (by him) that the people of Milan loved him, but apart from a rather paternalistic affection for his daughter, Miranda, there is little about Prospero that appeals. And when we meet Ariel and Caliban, we see that Prospero rules the island with a toxic combination of threatened violence and endlessly postponed promises of freedom – hardly the signs of a philosophical hermit accepting his advancing years with grace and wisdom. Yes, there's a certain mysticism about the part, but, played with alienation, a Brechtian performance would bring out Prospero's political role as an exiled and colonial despot, as much as the elegiac visionary of the romantic tradition.

Miranda presents the Brechtian director with further challenges. Above all, it is hard to know how to take her naivety seriously: we're told that she has lived her entire life on the island and not met any human other than her father and Caliban. As such she is, in some ways, a natural innocent, but her language and so much about her are that of a noble young aristocrat. The Brechtian director will find it hard to show much that is three dimensional or dialectical about Miranda, who is hardly a piece of Shakespearean 'raw material'. In the long first scene with her father, she expresses her concern about 'those that I saw suffer' (1.2.6) on the wrecked ship – the 'poor souls' who, she imagines, 'perished' (9) – and reprimands her father, but is less tolerant of Caliban whom, she claims, she taught how to speak (355). She even expresses what can be regarded as one of the more unappealing phrases in Shakespeare when she insists that Caliban's 'vile race / ... had that in't which good natures / Could not abide to be with' (359–61). Even if 'race' didn't quite carry the modern meaning, the sense of a person who by their very nature is to be abhorred hardly speaks of the all-embracing power of love.

It is, of course, Miranda's instant attraction to Prince Ferdinand – and her quick determination to be his wife – that is the chief action of Miranda's story and which, perhaps, most tests a modern audience's patience. Ferdinand is soon engaged in physical labour carrying logs, and a political production might explore not just his suitability for manual labour but the deforestation that is its result, as well as the purposes to which it is being done. We might also notice that this quite possibly bare-shirted muscular activity is fundamental to his appeal and recognize that aristocratic matches are rooted in the same erotic connections that affect 'ordinary' people. But this is, above all, a dynastic marriage and not one that a popular audience can appreciate personally.

And so, one of the chief questions is how much the Brechtian director should alienate this central triangle. Prospero is sufficiently complex for a production to lay bare his contradictions and conflicts, and Ferdinand can be seen as an experienced young nobleman who falls for an innocent young girl. It is Miranda who, I think, will cause the director most difficulties: How can we be helped to engage with her story in a way which does more than merely offer an idealized (and deeply sexist) projection of female naivety?

'This Rough Magic'

The Tempest's self-conscious theatricality can well be conceived of as 'Brechtian'. Indeed, David Barnett tells us of the argument that 'Prospero offers himself as an epic narrator who continually interrupts the action with explanation and commentary; that the diverse styles of the scenes invite different modes of views; and that Caliban in particular draws attention to this own use of language, making it worthy of careful consideration from the audience' (2013, 118).

The Philosopher in the *Messingkauf* is asked about 'fantastical plays':

> You should treat them as reports of dreams or sketches where the playwrights are likewise manipulating reality. Even if you have to try to establish what might have been, what the intention behind their story might have been and so on, you'll still have a lot of leeway.
>
> (*BoP*, 2014, 50)

In other words, *The Tempest* offers an intensely imaginative vision, allowing the modern director considerable space to create, intervene and amend. Indeed, it's hard to think of a Shakespeare play more in need of critical intervention if it is to resonate with a diverse modern audience. For it's surely possible to imagine a production relying on the theatre's 'rough magic' (5.1.50) to engage with the complex discussion about aesthetics that the play presents.

The Brechtian director, however, would insist that such an approach is allied to a coherent analysis of the political debates that are so central to the play's meaning. The tantalizing prospect, which I don't think I've ever seen, is a production which uses Brechtian means to stimulate the imagination and explore its role in human life, while also laying bare the play's knotty debates about power and ownership, equality and dignity, freedom and servitude.

In his *Journal* Brecht gives us a vivid sense of exactly this, as he describes the actor Charles Laughton reading *The Tempest* aloud in his house in Los Angeles:

> He sits cross-legged on a white sofa in front of a magnificent Bavarian baroque long-case clock so that all you can see is his Buddha-like belly, and he reads the play from a little book, partly like an actor, laughing at the jokes and excusing himself here and there for not getting a scene quite right. His reading leads me to see Prospero like that remarkable portrait of Napoleon on

St Helena, wearing a straw hat, with a yellow complexion and looking like a Dutch planter.

(*J*, 1993, 309)

I don't find this passage particularly illuminating, although portraying Prospero as a scruffy Napoleon is a good way of reminding us that he is a powerful man in exile. It also suggests the scale of the imaginative spark that the play can strike. Brecht adds that Laughton read Caliban 'with pity'. The Brechtian director would do well to attempt something similar, if their production is to engage with the world-historical catastrophes of slavery, racism and colonialism.

Provocations, Exercises and Practical Suggestions

- Draw up as precise a chronology as you can of the 'backstory' of the play, with particular emphasis on Prospero's arrival on the island. Improvise everyday life under Prospero's rule: who does what, when and where?
- How can we present *The Tempest* as a play concerned with slavery and colonialism? How much does it need to be altered if Caliban is to be played as an African slave working on a plantation in the Caribbean? And how could we show the island as having belonged to Caliban but now colonized by Prospero?
- Describe the various political views of the shipwrecked aristocrats and experiment with different ways of making them evident in the theatre.
- Study all the working people in the play (Stephano, Trinculo, Caliban, Ariel and the Boatswain) and see what they have in common, but also what divides them. Line them up by their position in the hierarchy. Describe the dangers they pose to their 'betters', and explore the reasons for their lack of success in creating a better future. How much does the play need to be changed in order to create greater political potency among these characters?

- Read the scenes between Prospero and Miranda and between Miranda and Ferdinand, and see whether there are any indications of Miranda resisting either her father or the prince. Should an actress play her simply as the naïve victim of patriarchal rage and domination, and does her relationship with Ferdinand offer a better future, or more of the same? Discuss how these options could be made visible.
- Imagine staging the play on an open stage in period costumes and hardly any props. What would that feel like?
- Consider the future of the island after the colonizers leave. Write a short epilogue (a song, perhaps) for Caliban finally celebrating his freedom.

PART FOUR

Questions and Suggestions

'He Made Suggestions'

Brecht described his own plays as 'attempts' (*Versuche*), written for the decade, not for eternity. Indeed, in one of his best short poems, he declared that when he died he 'needed no gravestone', but that if one was required, it should read, 'He made suggestions. We / Carried them out' (*P*, 1976, 126). The fact that his tomb in the Dorotheenstadt Cemetery in Berlin simply bears his surname shouldn't invalidate this emphasis on the provisional nature of artistic production.

And so, in this final chapter, I will pose three questions that the Brechtian director should answer in approaching a Shakespeare play, and then offer ten suggestions about how they might set about putting them into practice. Taken together these will, I hope, give a flavour of what it means to work within Brecht's circle of attention, and stimulate further inquiry, action and innovation.

There are, of course, no final answers, no reliable blueprint and open-minded curiosity must inform all our work. For if we learn one thing from Brecht it is that everything is in a permanent state of flux: after all, as the Greek philosopher Heraclitus insisted, 'you can't step twice into the same river'. But we should also consider Walter Benjamin's 'angel of history', who looked backwards into the abyss of the past, even as she moved forward into an unknown future. And this is the angel we have to wrestle with as we confront the legacy of the mighty Shakespeare and try to stage his plays today.

Three Questions

Why?

The Brechtian director of Shakespeare must ask themselves why they are presenting the play today, and whether an old work from such an alien world can say anything meaningful about the way that we live now. The director will need to explain why their revival justifies the theatre's efforts and what the modern audience will take from watching it.

But how would they go about this?

They might start by considering why the play isn't best left on the shelf. There are scores of Early Modern plays that we never stage: Why do this one? After all, it was created in a very different time from our own, and its meaning has changed continuously in the four centuries since it was written. And so they should examine how the play dramatizes social and political change and consider how modern audiences can best be helped to engage with such change, and, by extension, sense how change can happen today.

The director should remember that as the world changes, audiences change – and continue to change. Indeed, they might consider that just as Brecht's reading of *Coriolanus* developed as Germany moved beyond Hitler and grappled with the Cold War, so the meanings of all old plays evolve according to the time in which they are being revived. For the fact is, as Peter Brook insisted, one text may seem startlingly resonant one year, while another is slipping away into history. Shakespeare's 'contemporaneity' – that sense of a play, even a single line in a play, stepping out of its historic context and slapping you in the face – is a constantly evolving business. And so, the answers to why the play is being revived will keep evolving too.

Thus, as we've seen, *Measure for Measure*, with its story of the abuse of power for sexual purposes, seems to be a play for today, but may feel quite different soon. Similarly, *Timon of Athens*, with its depiction of the enormous divisions in wealth and privilege, feels peculiarly relevant as the gaps between the rich and the poor yawn ever wider, and unfettered capitalism rapes the very earth from which its wealth and resources sprang, but this resonance, could, with luck, fade. Likewise, a fresh conversation about the knotty contradictions in *The Merchant of Venice* has informed at least two recent British productions and the crowd of hungry protesters in the opening scene of *Coriolanus* should strike a chord in modern Britain, where an astounding 10 million people are reliant on foodbanks, but who knows what the future holds?

The crucial point is to engage in the conflicts that drive the play, and not plump for mere parallels: resonance should be found in the play's story, and if the director can persuade audiences to engage with that, and the changes that are brought about, in an attentive and thoughtful way, it stands the best chance of springing back to life.

But what should the director try to show?

What?

A play by Shakespeare, Brecht insisted, is the product of a specific historical moment. It dramatizes the clash not just of individuals and classes, but ideas and ways of doing things. Drama is the most dialectical of art forms and Shakespeare's plays embody the conflicts and contradictions of his time. And so, a Brechtian director will aim to do more than simply represent individuals, they'll try to catch the stuff of history itself.

The representation of conflict should be dramatized in individual experience, but the director shouldn't imagine that any single character can represent any of the conflicting forces alone. Instead (as in life), each one has a relationship to the group to which he or she belongs, and the character's relationship to the changing world is complex. As a result, the director will remember that human beings are a mixture of contradictory behaviours and attitudes, and will do everything they can to present the characters in the most vivid, three-dimensional and contradictory way imaginable.

Because of Brecht's desire to make the theatre a place for political debate, it's tempting to imagine that his vision of Shakespeare relied on clear political commentary. But Shakespeare offered Brecht the opposite of such journalistic thinking: instead, the 'great realist' shovelled unvarnished 'raw material' onto the stage, events and individuals taken straight from the street, and eschewed the kind of tidy editorializing that is so often the curse of the modern political theatre. Real people engaged in real-life struggles don't fit into tidy boxes, and Brecht, like Shakespeare, embraced the fact.

Further, the director will recognize that the changes generated by action are not always positive, certainly not always progressive. Indeed, many of the most dynamic and charismatic figures (Edmund in *King Lear*, for example, or Iago in *Othello*) have a destructive impact on the lives of other people. And both conservative figures like Adam in *As You Like It* and radical ones like Jack Cade in *Henry VI Part Two* look back to a golden age in the past even as they dream of a better future. Thus, Brecht's Shakespeare shows that social and political change is a complicated process, with contradictory outcomes. The crucial thing is for the director to show the characters engaged in such a process, whatever the outcome might be.

Crucially, the play's arguments are observed in the working out of the story. Dramatizing individuals coming into conflict with each other is the best way of showing how the world works, but also how it changes. And this includes the way that they talk, joke, make love and scrap with each other. For such a dialectical process, Brecht insists, is messy and difficult, public and private, political and cultural, and all too often causes pain and suffering, but, step by step, moment by moment, it leads to change. Even a drama as bleak as *King Lear* shows the possibility of resistance: 'the audacity of hope', indeed.

If, as Martin Luther King insisted, 'the arc of the moral universe is long, but it bends towards justice', Shakespeare as read by Brecht suggests that a better future is possible. This shouldn't be misinterpreted as easy: two steps forward and one step backwards are common, but so also are one forward and two back. For, as liberals who quote King sometimes forget, this will almost certainly require a fight – which may be violent, will certainly be painful – and Shakespeare dramatizes that bitter fact.

Brecht advised us not to 'start with the good old things but the bad new ones', but any approach to Shakespeare should explore the bad things of his own time (Jameson, 1977, 106). This, then, will help us illuminate the 'bad new ones' of our own time. The new is historically circumscribed, partial and provisional, but it is not to be denied. And this is fundamental to what the Brechtian director wants to suggest.

How?

If we know what we want to show, how can we realize it in the theatre?

The key is to do everything we can to ensure that the audience engages with the drama itself: with the actions being presented, the arguments, the interactions and the change that the story enacts. The problem with the conventional theatre, Brecht noticed, is that it 'theatres everything down'; instead, the modern audience should be prompted into engaging with the world beyond the stage door. Paradoxically, that requires an approach which draws attention to the fact that what is being presented is an artifice, but it is an artifice which has its sights firmly set on reality. This was the opposite of the poisonous theatricality of the Nazi Nuremberg rallies which swept its audience up in an emotional frenzy, with no truthful relationship with the world beyond.

Because Shakespeare's plays are products of a different world, Brecht wanted the director to grant them historical distance. At the same time, however, he wanted the play to be performed in a way that can be readily understood by the modern audience, and deploy a kind of verbal, physical and theatrical energy which allows audiences to engage directly. In other words, the director should frame the distinctly historicized events in such a way that we're invited to compare it with our own experiences.

Although the acting should convey emotion and be fully charged, the audience's sympathy should be checked and the actions of the mighty scrutinized. We should be shown the impact of their actions on those who serve them (and are often oppressed by them). Each moment should be carefully articulated and the characters' behaviour should be made clear. The production should be rational and clear, focused and objective, but also heartfelt and earthy, passionate and engaged. Such clarity is best achieved by a suggestive simplicity in the setting and a crisp focus on the figures themselves, presented in continuous and ever-changing relationships with each other.

To do this the actors and the creative team must think for themselves. Above all, they need to attend to the play's unvarnished 'raw material', whether in the text or in the world in which we live, and present it in all its contradictory, dialectical, energy. And that lies at the heart of our responsibility not just to the theatre but to our fellow human beings.

Ten Suggestions

As the world changes, our views of Shakespeare change. Indeed, many of the conflicts that Shakespeare dramatized so vividly 400 years ago seem even more remote today than they did to Brecht. This is exacerbated by the fact that modern progressives often identify with causes largely unaddressed by Brecht, whose preoccupations were labour and capital, power and exploitation. And so, Brecht needs to be historicized just as Shakespeare does, and we shouldn't imagine that everything he wrote is valuable. Consequently, we need to pick our way through his writings with a mixture of respect and scepticism, an open mind and a questioning spirit.

And it's with this that I offer ten tentative suggestions addressed to the director who has committed themself to staging a play by Shakespeare in the Brechtian fashion.

1. Develop an interest in the details of what happens in the drama and take nothing for granted. Find ways of presenting the events as clearly as possible and do everything you can to entertain by dramatizing disagreement and conflict, in big things and little. Above all, tell the story, and make telling the story your guiding star.

2. Communicate the process of continuous change. Make sure that the actors don't play the end of the play at the beginning (Lear isn't mad at the outset; Romeo starts the play in love with another girl, and so) and plot these developments as accurately as you can. Help the audience see how the characters change, but also how society changes.

3. Resist simplistic notions of an impersonal fate. Don't present anything as inevitable and try to show the impact of individual decisions and actions. Focus, above all, on those moments when a character chooses to do one thing instead of another, and do whatever you can to show how he or she came to that decision, as well as its consequences.

4. Explore what happens *between* the characters and present human beings as social animals in a continual prices of interaction. Yes, they have inner thoughts, but these express their relationships with other people. Remember throughout that presenting the way that people live alongside each other is the fundamental objective of the theatre.

5. Recognize that social class exists and that the discrepancies in power, wealth and status are vast. Look for those moments when class differences are at their most pronounced, while simultaneously exploring the contradictions within classes. Remember that character is created by social circumstances – background, education and wealth – and clarify these wherever they show their head.

6. Explore the contradictions within the world of the play and show how different it is from ours. Embrace historical difference and aim to dramatize the core conflicts which define the historical moment. And explore the contradictions in the characters: kind and cruel, visionary and blind, radical and conservative, all at the same time. Relish the presentation of such contradiction and see it as central to Shakespeare's realism.

7. Don't treat the text as an unalterable monolith and try not to be mesmerized by its status. Remember that there is no law saying that you must not amend Shakespeare, but attend to the details of what is in front of you, its beauties and quirks, and follow closely its many shifts in tone and register. Make sure that the actors' approach to the text is rooted in real life and avoid the air of mystery still common in some Shakespearean acting.

8. Show the way that material objects shape lives and ensure that the props and the costumes, the furniture and the paperwork, have a three-dimensionality to them, a sense

of history and status. Let the props – the crown, a book, a mirror and so on – carry their own metaphorical meaning, but also explore the way the characters interact with objects in specific ways according to their social circumstances. Employ the minimum of scenery, simply to suggest time and place, and ensure that whatever is used is informed by its social purpose. Above all ensure that people are at the heart of the composition.

9. Organize the action in such a way that the audience can grasp what is happening between the characters, action by action, moment by moment. Arrange the figures so that they express physically the essential social relationships. Ensure that these physical, gestural relationships constantly evolve. And try to make them attractive and stylish.

10. Bring a combination of sophistication and naiveté to your work and honour Brecht's insistence that 'the dramatist needs to be able to look at the complex world with wonder' (Barnett, 2013, 115). Above all, be simple and clear. In Shakespearean theatre then, as in life.

REFERENCES

Note on the Quotations

All quotations from Shakespeare are taken from Arden Shakespeare, mostly the Third Series.

Confusingly, there are two different editions of *Brecht on Theatre* (1964 and 2015). Although the later volume has some new material, some of the same passages are repeated but in fresh translations. I mostly cite the 1964 edition but occasionally refer to the 2015 edition for essays omitted from the original edition.

Brecht dispensed with capital letters in his *Journals*. I have reinstated them here for ease of reading. With apologies to Brecht and his scrupulous English editors.

Primary

Brecht, B. *Brecht on Art and Politics* (2003), eds. T. Kuhn & S. Giles (Bloomsbury. London) [*BAP, 2003*].
Brecht, B. *Brecht on Performance* (2014), eds. T. Kuhn, S. Giles & M. Silberman (Bloomsbury. London) [*BoP, 2014*].
Brecht, B. *Brecht on Theatre* (1964), trans. J. Willett (Bloomsbury. London) [*BoT, 1964*].
Brecht, B. *Brecht on Theatre* (2015), eds. M. Silberman, S. Giles & T. Kuhn, trans. various (Bloomsbury. London) [*BoT, 2015*].
Brecht, B. *Collected Plays* (Bloomsbury. London) [*CP*].
Brecht, B. *Diaries 1920–1922* (1979), trans. J. Willett, ed. H. Ramthun (Bloomsbury. London) [*D, 1979*].
Brecht, B. *Journals 1934–1955* (1993), trans. H. Rorrison, ed. J. Willett (Bloomsbury. London) [*J, 1993*].
Brecht, B. *Letters 1913–1956* (1990), trans. R. Manheim, ed. J. Willett (Bloomsbury. London) [*L, 1990*].

Brecht, B. *Messingkauf Dialogues* (1965), trans. J. Willett (Bloomsbury. London) [*MD*, 1965].
Brecht, B. *Poems 1913–1956* (1976), eds. J. Willett & R. Manheim, trans. various (Bloomsbury. London) [*P*, 1976].

Secondary

Auden, W. H. (2000), *Lectures on Shakespeare* (Princeton University Press. Princeton, NJ).
Auerbach, E. (1946, trans. 1953), *Mimesis*, trans. W. R. Trask (Princeton University Press. Princeton, NJ).
Baldwin, J. (1964), 'Why I Stopped Hating Shakespeare' in *The Cross of Redemption: Uncollected Writings*, ed. R. Kenan (Pantheon, New York, NY), pp. 53–6.
Barnett, D. (2013), 'Brecht as Great Shakespearean: A Lifelong Connection' in Volume XIV of Arden's *Great Shakespeareans* series, ed. R. Morse (Bloomsbury. London).
Barnett, D. (2015a), *Brecht in Practice: Theatre, Theory and Performance* (Bloomsbury. London).
Barnett, D. (2015b), *A History of the Berliner Ensemble* (Cambridge University Press. Cambridge).
Bartolovich, C., D. Hillman & J. Howard (2012), eds. *Great Shakespeareans: Marx and Freud* (Bloomsbury. London).
Bate, J. (1992), ed. *The Romantics on Shakespeare* (Penguin. London).
Benjamin, W. (1970), *Illuminations*, ed. H. Arendt, trans H. Zohn (Verso. London).
Benjamin, W. (1998), *Understanding Brecht*, trans. A. Bostock (Verso. London).
Berry, R. (1977), *On Directing Shakespeare: Interviews with Contemporary Directors* (Routledge. London).
Bloom, H. (1999), *Shakespeare: The Invention of the Human* (Fourth Estate. London).
Brook, P. (1968), *The Empty Space* (Penguin. London).
Brook, P. (2013), *The Quality of Mercy: Reflections on Shakespeare* (Nick Hern Books. London).
Carlson, H., Tenschert, J., Weigel, H. & Wekwerth, M. 'Dialogue: Berliner Ensemble' *Tulane Drama Review*, vol.12, no.1 (Cambridge), pp. 112–17.
Cavell, S. (2003), *Disowning Knowledge in Seven Plays of Shakespeare* (Cambridge University Press. Cambridge).

Césaire, A. (2009), *Une Tempête*, trans. P. Crispin, cited in M. Garber (Pantheon. New York, NY), pp. 528–34.
Coleridge, S. T. (1992), 'Literary Remains' in *The Romantics on Shakespeare*, ed. J. Bate (Penguin. London).
Dollimore, J. (1984), *Radical Tragedy: Religion, Ideology and Power in the Drama of Shakespeare and His Contemporaries* (Harvester Press. Brighton).
Dollimore, J. & A. Sinfield (1985), eds. *Political Shakespeare: Essays in Cultural Materialism* (Manchester University Press. Manchester).
Ewen, F. (1967), *Bertolt Brecht: His Life, His Art, His Times* (Citadel Press. New York, NY).
Fitter, C. (2012), *Radical Shakespeare: Politics and Stagecraft in the Early Career* (Routledge. Abingdon).
Fitter, C. (2017), ed. *Shakespeare and the Politics of Commoners* (Oxford University Press. Oxford).
Fuegi, J. (1987), *Bertolt Brecht: Chaos, according to Plan* (Cambridge University Press. Cambridge).
Fuegi, J. (1994), *The Life and Lies of Bertolt Brecht* (Harper Collins. London).
Gill, P. (2008), *Apprenticeship* (Oberon Books. London).
Granville Barker, H. (1993), *Prefaces to Shakespeare* (Nick Hern Books. London).
Grass, G. (1966), *Plays*, trans. R. Manheim (Penguin. Harmondsworth).
Hale, J. (1993), *The Civilisation of Europe in the Renaissance* (Harper Perennial. New York, NY).
Hayman, R. (1983), *Brecht: A Biography* (Oxford University Press. Oxford).
Hazlitt, W. (1908), *Characters of Shakespeare's Plays* (Cambridge University Press. Cambridge).
Heinemann, M. (1992), 'Demystifying the Mystery of State: *King Lear* and the World Upside Down' in *Shakespeare Survey*, ed. S. Wells, XLIV (Cambridge University Press. Cambridge), pp. 75–83.
Heinemann, M. (1994, second ed.), 'How Brecht Read Shakespeare' in *Political Shakespeare: Essays in Cultural Materialism*, eds. J. Dollimore & A. Sinfield (Manchester University Press. Manchester), pp. 226–54.
Hobgood, A. (2021), *Beholding Disability in Renaissance England* (University of Michigan Press. Ann Arbor, MI).
Jameson, F. (1977), ed. *Aesthetics and Politics* (Verso. London).
Kettle, A. (1964), ed. *Shakespeare in a Changing World* (Lawrence & Wishart. London).
Kiernan, V. (1993), *Shakespeare: Poet and Citizen* (Verso. London).
Kiernan, V. (1996), *Eight Tragedies of Shakespeare* (Verso. London).

Kleber, P. & C. Visser (1991), *Re-interpreting Brecht: His Influence on Contemporary Drama and Film* (Cambridge University Press. Cambridge).

Kott, J. (1964), *Shakespeare Our Contemporary*, trans. B. Taborski (Methuen. London).

Kozintsev, G. (1977), *King Lear: The Space of Tragedy* (Heinemann. London).

Lukács, G. (1963), *The Meaning of Contemporary Realism* (Merlin Press. London).

O'Toole, F. (2002), *Shakespeare Is Hard, but so Is Life: A Radical Guide to Shakespearian Tragedy* (Granta Books. London).

Ormsby, R. (2014), *Coriolanus, Shakespeare in Performance* (Manchester University Press. Manchester).

Parker, S. (2014), *Bertolt Brecht: A Literary Life* (Bloomsbury. London).

Patterson, A. (1989), *Shakespeare and the Popular Voice* (Oxford University Press. Oxford).

Reynolds, B. (2003), '"What Is the City but the People?" Transversal Performance and Radical Politics in Shakespeare's *Coriolanus* and Brecht's *Coriolan*' in *Performing Transversally: Reimagining Shakespeare and the Critical Future*, ed. B. Reynolds (Palgrave Macmillan. London), pp. 85–110.

Rosen, M. (2004), *William Shakespeare: In His Times, for Our Times* (Granta Books. London).

Ryan, K. (1995), *Shakespeare* (Harvester Wheatsheaf. Hemel Hempstead).

Ryan, K. (2015), *Shakespeare's Universality: Here's Fine Revolution* (Bloomsbury. London).

Smith, E. (2020), *This Is Shakespeare: How to Read the World's Greatest Playwright* (Penguin. London).

Thompson, E. P. (1963), *The Making of the English Working Class* (Victor Gollancz. London).

Unwin, S. (2005), *A Guide to the Plays of Bertolt Brecht* (Methuen. London).

Unwin, S. (2014), *The Complete Brecht Toolkit* (Nick Hern Books. London).

Unwin, S. (2022), *Poor Naked Wretches: Shakespeare's Working People* (Reaktion Books. London).

Weimann, R. (1978), *Shakespeare and the Popular Tradition in the Theater: Studies in the Social Dimension of Dramatic Form and Function*, ed. R. Schwartz (John Hopkins University Press. Baltimore, MD).

Wekwerth, M. (2012), *Daring to Play: A Brecht Companion* (Bloomsbury. London).

Willems, M. (2010), ed. *Great Shakespeareans: Voltaire, Goethe, Schlegel, Coleridge* (Bloomsbury. London).
Willett, J. (1977), *The Theatre of Bertolt Brecht: A Study from Eight Aspects* (Methuen. London).
Willett, J. (1984), *Brecht in Context* (Methuen. London).
Witt, H. (1975), ed. *Brecht as They Knew Him*, trans. J. Peet (Lawrence & Wishart. London).

INDEX

Abel 125
Actium 84
Adam 82
Adorno, Theodor 113
alienation, (alienation effect) 67, 74–80, 89, 102, 115, 120, 122, 126, 128, 130, 141–2, 159, 162, 167, 173, 183
America (American) 4, 11–12, 95, 135, 166, 169, 177
Anglican 149
Annunciation, The 143
Antony and Cleopatra 35, 55, 84, 103, 130
    Antony 31, 35, 42, 103
    Cleopatra 31
    Octavia 35, 103
Arden, Forest of 125, 127–8, 130
Aristotle 14, 25, 68
Artaud, Antonin 24
Arturo Ui, The Resistible Rise of 111–13
    Cabbage Trust 112
    Dullfeet, Betty 112
    Ui, Arturo 112–13, 122
As You Like It 36, 45, 93, 110, 125–34, 195
    Adam 126–7, 130, 132–3, 195
    Celia 127, 129, 131, 133
    Charles the Wrestler 132
    Corin 128, 133
    Frederick, Duke 125, 127, 129–30
    Hymen 132, 134
    Jacques 130, 134
    Le Beau 126
    Oliver 125, 129, 131, 133
    Orlando 125–7, 130–4
    Phoebe 51, 65, 129, 131–4
    Rosalind 51, 65, 71–2, 127, 131–4
    Senior, Duke 127, 130–1
    Silvius 51, 129, 131
    Touchstone 127–8, 132–4
Auerbach, Erich 18, 40

Bacon, Francis 56
Baldwin, James 89–90
Barnett, David 14, 17–18, 28, 39, 41, 44, 53, 62–3, 65, 67, 91, 95, 105, 107, 112, 165–6, 171–2, 184, 199
Barton, John 3, 54
Benjamin, Walter 14, 24, 27, 80, 145, 191
Berghaus, Ruth 172
Berlin 4, 12–14, 19, 25, 61, 120, 160, 165–6, 189
Berliner Ensemble, the 5, 13, 17, 54, 62, 66, 69, 101, 105, 139, 163, 172
Besson, Benno 5, 67
Bible, biblical 16, 51, 68, 71, 88, 94, 122, 126, 143
Bloom, Harold 84
Bouffes du Nord 4
Boyd, Michael 4
Brandes, Georg 166

Brecht on Performance (BoP)
14–16, 31, 34, 38–9, 42–3,
48–50, 56, 75, 82, 86, 92–3,
100, 116–17, 137, 152–3,
155, 160–1, 185
Brecht on Theatre (BoT) 14–15,
24–6, 28–33, 40, 42, 44,
48–9, 52, 56, 65–8, 71,
73–83, 88, 92, 94–5, 97,
99–100, 102–4, 106–7, 115,
162, 167
Bridge Theatre 3
Brook, Peter 4–5, 24, 36, 53,
162–4, 179, 191
Büchner, Georg 13, 16
Danton's Death 16
Woyzeck 16
Buddha 185
Busch, Ernst 65, 172

Cain 125
Cambridge, University of 3
Caribbean 186
Carroll, William 18
Catholic, Catholicism 29, 51, 146,
149
Caucasian Chalk Circle, The 95,
126–7
Cavell, Stanley 166
Césaire, Aimé 179
La Tempête 179
Chaplin, Charlie 16
Christ (Christian) 57, 98, 156
Cockney 133
Coleridge, Samuel Taylor 181
Copenhagen 135
Coriolan 94, 170–2, 174
Coriolanus 15, 46, 54, 56–8, 65,
94, 100, 110, 149, 165–75,
193–4
citizens (plebeians) 165–8,
170–1, 173–4
Martius (Coriolanus) 42,
167–74

Menenius 167, 171
Virgilia 170, 175
Volumnia 169–70, 175
Coward, Noel 19

Davies, Howard 4
Decision, The 26
Deutsches Theater 13
Dexter, John 3
Donnellan, Declan 4
Doran, Gregory 3
Dorotheenstadt Cemetery 189
Dover 158
Dromgoole, Dominic 3

Eastcheap 84
Edwardian 3
Elizabethan 3, 30, 40, 42, 75–6,
81, 87, 89, 91–2, 99, 102,
111, 113–14, 129, 133, 137
Engel, Eric 165
Engels, Friedrich 128
England, English 3, 5, 13–14, 16,
18, 20, 29–30, 33, 42, 48,
54, 67–8, 76, 87, 89–90, 99,
102, 114–15, 125, 132, 136,
149, 152, 155, 163, 165,
170, 179, 182
epic 16, 48–50, 81, 110, 113, 129,
163, 165, 184
Ewen, Frederic 17, 79
Eyre, Richard 3

fabel 52–5, 61, 68, 98, 105, 175
Feuchtwanger, Lion 15
First World War 11, 99, 125
Fitter, Chris 18, 31, 165, 179
Florence 56
Francesca, Piero della 98
Frecknall, Rebecca 4

Galileo 56, 95, 103
Gaskill, William 3
Géricault, Théodore 98

INDEX

German 5, 16–18, 23–4, 29, 36, 75, 81, 87, 102, 105, 115, 135–6, 172
Germany 4
   East Germany 28, 165, 171, 191
   Imperial Germany 11, 25
   Nazi Germany 13–14
   Weimar Germany 12, 19, 25, 27
   West Germany 14, 165, 172, 174, 191
gestus, gest, gestic 71–4, 88–9, 97, 102, 119, 164
Gill, Peter 3, 119
Globe Theatre 3, 91–3, 100, 116, 153
Goethe, Johann van 13–14, 92
Goodbody, Buzz 4
Goold, Rupert 4
Granville Barker, Harley 3, 84, 99, 159
Grass, Günter
   Plebeians Rehearse the Uprising, The 173

Hagen, Uta 24
Hall, Peter 3, 24, 54
Hamlet 16, 47, 57, 64, 66, 76, 79, 89, 95, 100, 130
   Claudius 69, 72, 79
   Fortinbras's captain 79
   Gravedigger, the 64
   Guildenstern 83
   Hamlet 30–1, 42–3, 45, 47, 51, 64–5, 67, 69–70, 76, 78–9, 83, 99, 101
   Polonius 82
   Rosencrantz 83
   Yorick 64
Hastie, Rob 54
Hauptmann, Elisabeth 87, 102
Hazlitt, William 18, 182
Hegel, G. W. F. 29, 43, 95

Heinemann, Margot 16–19, 39, 46, 48–9, 53, 82, 115, 136–7, 147, 150, 153, 163, 168–9, 171
Henry IV, Parts One and Two 47, 54, 82, 84, 86
   Carriers 47
   Doll Tearsheet 82
   Douglas 86
   Falstaff, Sir John 82, 95
   Glendower, Owen 86
   Percies, the 86
   Quickly, Mistress 82
Henry V 30, 39, 65, 93
   Chorus 26, 93
   Williams 39
Henry VI, Parts One, Two and Three 3, 40, 46, 65, 75, 99, 114, 182, 193
   Buckingham, Duke of 99
   Cade, Jack 39, 46, 65, 99, 103, 182, 193
   Clifford, Old Lord 99
Hill-Gibbons, Joe 4
Hitler, Adolf 12, 25, 54, 85, 111, 115, 120, 160, 165, 172, 191
Hobgood, Alison 179, 182
Hollywood 12, 19, 27
Hytner, Nicholas 3

Icke, Robert 4
Italy 33

Jacobean 51, 57, 110, 149, 151–2, 155, 165
Johnson, Boris 123
Julius Caesar 41, 46, 54, 56, 58, 100, 171
   Brutus 38, 56
   Caesar 65

Kiernan, Victor 150
King, Martin Luther 193

King Lear 4, 14, 45, 57, 69–70,
    72–3, 77, 82, 96, 101, 103,
    110, 130, 149–64, 193
  Burgundy, Duke of 72
  Captain 149, 161–2
  Cordelia 69, 149, 152–3, 160,
    163
  Edgar 57, 149, 151, 155–6,
    159, 164
  Edmund 149–50, 155, 160–2,
    193
  First Servant 157–8, 164
  Fool, The 149–50, 155, 160, 164
  France, King of 72
  Gloucester, Earl of 72, 149–50,
    156–61, 163–4
  Goneril 149–50, 152, 154, 157
  Kent, Earl of 72, 149, 153–6,
    164
  Lear, King 153–4
  Oswald 149, 154–5
  Poor Tom 57, 155–6, 159
  Regan 44, 149–50, 152, 157, 161
Kleist, Heinrich von 13
  Broken Jug, The 105
  Adam, Judge 105
Kott, Jan 4, 36, 162, 173, 181
  *Shakespeare Our
    Contemporary* 36
Kozintsev, Grigori 162–3

Laughton, Charles 87, 125, 130,
  137, 153, 185–6
Lawson, Nigel 150
Leavis, FR 3
Lecoq, Jacques 24
Lee, Stewart 57
Lenz, Jakob 13
Littlewood, Joan 4
Lloyd, Phyllida 54
London 5, 33, 51, 56, 102, 133,
  137, 152, 165–6, 173
Los Angeles 12, 14, 185
Luther, Martin 16

Macbeth 16, 35, 47, 49, 53, 55,
    57, 83–4, 88, 95, 113
  Banquo 35, 53, 83–5
  Duncan 43, 55, 85
  Fleance 35, 84
  Lady Macbeth 84
  Lady Macduff 53, 85
  Macbeth 35, 42–3, 53, 55, 65,
    71, 85, 89, 182
  Macduff 52, 85, 88
  Malcolm 88, 95
  murderers 83
Manheim, Ralph 19
Marlowe, Christopher 15, 88
  Edward II 15–16, 88
Marx, Karl, Marxist 12, 14, 16,
  25, 29–30, 40, 81, 125, 128,
  150, 165, 168, 171
Massacre of the Innocents 85
McBurney, Simon 4
Measure for Measure 15, 36, 45,
    51, 58, 68–9, 77, 102, 110,
    135, 147, 194
  Abhorson 139
  Angelo 45, 69, 136–47
  Barnardine 139, 143
  Claudio 77, 137, 140–4,
    146–7
  Duke, the 77–8, 136–7, 142–6
  Friar Thomas 142
  Isabella 69, 77, 136–47
  Juliet 137
  Keepdown, Kate 138
  Lucio 143, 145
  Mariana 136, 142, 144–5,
    147
  Overdone, Mistress 138, 143,
    146
  Pompey 68, 138–9, 143, 146
  Provost 139, 143, 147
Meisner, Sanford 24
Mendes, Sam 3
Merchant of Venice, The 36, 50,
    57, 194

Merry Wives of Windsor 95
   Falstaff, Sir John 95
Messingkauf Dialogues, The 15,
   34, 38, 50, 82, 161, 185
Meyerhold, Vsevelod 24
Midlands Revolt 165
Midsummer Night's Dream, A
   4, 54, 58, 69, 86, 93, 96,
   100–1
   Egeus 86–7
   Hermia 86
   Theseus, Duke 86–7, 93
Mitchell, Stanley 80
'Mona Lisa' 104
Monasteries, Dissolution of 126
Moscow 149
Mother Courage and Her Children
   13, 66, 94–5, 100–1, 103,
   127, 138, 163, 169
Much Ado About Nothing 52, 54,
   58, 73–4, 79, 83, 86
   Beatrice 73–5, 79
   Benedick 73–5, 79
   Borachio 83
   Claudio 58, 74–5
   Conrade 83
   Don John 83
   Hero 73
   Leonato 86
Mussolini, Benito 33

Naples 182
National Socialists (Nazi) 13, 19,
   81, 106, 136, 172, 194
National Theatre 3–4
Neher, Caspar 94, 96, 170
New York Public Theatre 54
Noble, Adrian 4
Northumberland 86
Nunn, Trevor 3
Nuremberg 112, 194

Obama, Barack 67, 160
Observer, The 17

Othello 31, 42, 44, 193
   Iago 193
Otto, Teo 94

Paris 4
Parker, Stephen 13, 23, 48, 81,
   171–2
Parthia 84
Paterson, Annabel 18
Pericles 58
Piscator, Erwin 24
Puritan, Puritanism 45, 51, 86,
   137–8, 146
Putin, Vladimir 123

Renaissance 40, 51
Rice, Emma 4
Richard III 3, 47, 110–23
   citizens 119–20
   Clarence 47, 114, 117, 119,
   122
   Hastings 114, 120
   murderers 118–19, 122
   Richard III, King 31, 42, 55,
   113, 115–16, 121, 123
   Richmond 115, 117, 121
   Scrivener, the 120
   Tyrrel, James 120
Riverside Studios 4
Rome 84, 94, 96, 100, 133, 166,
   168–71, 175
Romeo and Juliet 47, 51, 67, 75,
   102, 125
   Friar, the 75
   Juliet 43, 51, 65, 67, 75,
   83
   musicians 47, 75
   Nurse, the 75
   Peter 75
   Romeo 43, 51, 75, 197
Round Heads and Pointed Heads
   15, 135–6
Royal Court Theatre 3–4

Royal Shakespeare Company
    (RSC) 3–4
Ryan, Kiernan 18
Rylands, George ('Dadie') 3

Salvation Army 16
Santa Monica 87, 125, 153
Scandinavia 4, 12, 15
Schall, Ekkehard 172–3
Schiffbauerdamm, Theater am 13
Schiller, Friedrich 47
    Mary Stuart 47
Schlegel, August 13
Scotland 86
Second World War 3, 126
Shapiro, James 157
'Short Organum for the Theatre'
    15, 65, 71
Shrewsbury 84
South America 135
Soviet Union 12
Spanish 75
St Clare, Sisterhood of 145
Stalin, Josef (Stalinist) 19, 28, 169,
    171–3
Stanislavski, Konstantin 24, 70
State Yiddish Theatre 149
Sternberg, Fritz 125
Strasberg, Lee 24, 95
Stratford East, Theatre Royal 4
Swedish 76
Switzerland 13, 15

Taming of the Shrew, The 33
Tempest, The 54, 96, 110,
    177–87
    Ariel 182–3, 186
    Boatswain, the 180–1, 186
    Caliban 177–87
    Ferdinand 183–4, 187
    Gonzalo 181
    Miranda 178, 183–4, 187
    Prospero 177–80, 182–7

Stephano 181–2, 186
Trinculo 181–2, 186
Tenschert, Joachim 95, 171–3
Thames, River 92, 95
Third Reich 28, 165
Thirty Years War 66
Threepenny Opera, The 138
Tieck, Ludwig 13
Timon of Athens 194
    Timon 31
Tower of London 114, 120
Tretyakov, Sergei 135
Trump, Donald 54, 67, 123
Twelfth Night 33, 86, 103
    Aguecheek, Sir Andrew 86
    Belch, Sir Toby 86
    Malvolio 86, 103

Valentin, Karl 16
van Hove, Ivo 4
Verona 51
Victorian 3, 18
Vienna 36, 138, 142, 145–7
Viertel, Bertold 135
Virgil 180
    Aeneid, The 180
von Appen, Karl 94

Wales 86
Wall Street Crash 12
Warner, Deborah 4
Wars of the Roses, The 3, 54
Webster, John 16
    Duchess of Malfi, The 16
Weigel, Helene 12, 66–7, 169, 173
Weimann, Robert 18, 51
Wekwerth, Manfred 115, 170–3
Willett, John 15, 19, 67, 128, 173
Wilson Knight, G 162
Wilson, Richard 18

Zola, Emile 25, 37, 48